D0178436

SCENT IN
THE GARDEN

SCENT IN THE GARDEN

FRANCES PERRY

PHOTOGRAPHS BY
DENI BOWN

CASSELL

FRONTISPIECE:

An old Bourbon rose - the fragrant
'Madame Isaac Pereire' - growing
alongside sweet-scented pinks

Cassell Publishers Limited
Villiers House, 41/47 Strand
London WC2N 5JE

First paperback edition 1992
First published in 1989 by Webb & Bower (Publishers) Ltd

British Library Cataloguing-in-Publication Data

A catalogue record for this book is available
from the British Library

ISBN 0 304 34211 4
Designed by Peter Wrigley
Original edition produced by
Justin Knowles Publishing Group
Exeter

This edition produced by
New Cavendish Books Limited
3 Denbigh Road
London W11 2SJ

Typeset in Great Britain by Keyspools Ltd
Printed and bound in Hong Kong

CONTENTS

INTRODUCTION   7

A HISTORY OF PERFUME   9

THE USES OF SCENTED PLANTS   21

THE RELEASE OF SCENTS   27

THE FRAGRANT GARDEN   37

SPRING FRESHNESS   47

SUMMER'S BOUNTY   69

AUTUMN RIPENESS   121

WINTERSWEET   137

SCENTED RECIPES   149

A SELECTION OF FRAGRANT PLANTS   153

INDEX   159

INTRODUCTION

Narcissus 'Paper White'
OPPOSITE: Ghent azaleas

'ANYTHING GREEN that grew out of the mold, was an excellent herb to our fathers of old' wrote Rudyard Kipling, but who can tell when plants were first cultivated primarily for fragrance?

It is reasonably safe to assume that scents have been appreciated since the dawn of time. Smell is an indefinable sense, closely associated with taste, so that the two are frequently linked – a circumstance exploited by clever cooks in gourmet dishes. Gardeners also have long been aware of the evocative quality of flower fragrance and it is a poor garden that fails to make the most of this extra quality.

Gardeners worldwide share a love of fragrant plants. In New Orleans I noticed scented azaleas and oleanders growing in many gardens and wondered how they survived the heat of late summer. My hostess explained that old New Orleans had inherited the Spanish love of fragrance and since so much of their leisure was spent out of doors, people worked hard at their gardens. Because the plants had no rest period, almost all the trees remained evergreen, but with the aid of shade and cooling fountains they flourished, with the result that roses, night-blooming jasmine with its penetrating fragrance, and even narcissi thrived in their shelter.

Not all plant scents are alike in flavour or intensity. They can be strong or delicate, invasive or subtle according to their nature or the part of the plant which produces the perfume – be it flowers, leaves, roots, gum, bark, fruits, or wood. Again, some flowers smell strongest at sunrise, others around midday or in the dead of night.

Nor is the size or freshness of the flower the determining factor regarding the quality or quantity of plant scents. Some sweet-smelling flowers are very small, even petal-less, while others release their scents only after a time, usually during a breakdown of tissue following harvesting.

In making a scented garden, we are fortunate in having plenty of fragrant plants from which to choose. There are representatives for most garden features, for example shrubberies, annual beds, herbaceous borders, rock gardens, and ponds; some are suitable for growing indoors; and some can act as substitutes for grass in lawns.

A HISTORY
OF PERFUME

Rosa gallica officinalis

A LTHOUGH PERFUMES seem to have been appreciated in many countries and over a long period of time, the earliest authenticated evidence of their importance comes from Egypt, where hieroglyphics and symbols on murals and monuments indicate the use of fragrant spices from around 2600–2100 BC. This period was known as the Pyramid Age, when some 100,000 labourers employed in building Cheops' great pyramid were apparently kept fit enough to work with diets which included medicinal herbs, onions, and garlic.

A monument erected in honour of the pharaoh Sahure during the same period (circa 2500 BC) records the importation of huge quantities of gold, ebony, and silver and of 80,000 measures of myrrh from Punt (present-day Somalia). A few centuries later, in 1485 BC, following population growth and with myrrh increasingly needed for fumigation and embalming, the queen of Egypt, Hatshepsut, sent five sailing vessels and a miscellany of collectors to Punt to bring back living specimens of incense-bearing trees to grow in the gardens of Thebes. This probably makes her one of the world's first known plant collectors. Although the trees eventually failed they did survive for a time in this alien territory.

The reason for their importance was largely that in ancient times unpleasant odours were associated with evil, whereas clean, sweet scents were linked with goodness and purity. Egyptian upper classes regularly fumigated their homes with incense and pleasantly scented herbs, partly for enjoyment but also to counteract the unpleasant odours of humanity. This was also the principle lying behind embalming, when the stomach contents were removed and the corpse cleaned with sweet-smelling herbs and strewn with fragrant, long-lasting plants and spices.

Particularly important substances were myrrh and frankincense, both of which were included in the precious gifts presented to the infant Jesus by the Magi (Matthew 2:11). Myrrh was obtained from *Commiphora myrrha*, a small thorny evergreen tree, native to Abyssinia, southern Arabia, and Somalia, whose bark emitted clear yellow droplets with a strong and persistent perfume. At times similar globules fell from the glandular hairs of the foliage and were caught in the beards of goats browsing in the undergrowth, to be collected, when solidified, by Arab goatherds – a practice that has existed since the time of Solomon. Myrrh is little used today.

A 16th-century illustration showing frankincense gum being collected as it oozes from the bark of *Boswellia* trees

Frankincense is obtained from various species of *Boswellia* – smooth-barked trees with lemon-scented, ash-like foliage and greenish-white, star-shaped flowers. It occurs naturally as yellow droplets of gum resin oozing from the bark or its production can be artificially stimulated by making incisions in the wood.

Because frankincense burns readily and has such a pleasant scent it was – and still is – in great demand as incense. When it is burned phenol (carbolic acid) is produced, so it may have had an antiseptic effect also. Certainly it was an important article of trade in the ancient world – Phoenician merchants grew rich upon it and it became southern Arabia's most important source of wealth. It was also among the gifts of spices, perfumes, gold, and jewels brought by the queen of Sheba to King Solomon in the 10th century BC.

Cinnamon, another ancient spice, indigenous to India and Ceylon and long used in the Orient, is produced from the bark of a bushy tree called *Cinnamomum zeylanicum*. The bark is peeled from

The leathery leaves of *Cinnamon zeylanicum*, the tree from whose bark cinnamon is produced

the shoots, and left to dry for a day. Then the outer bark is stripped away, leaving the inner bark, which, as it dries, rolls up into a quill. Smaller quills are fitted inside larger ones and they all, when thoroughly dried, curl up together. This is the most valuable form of cinnamon, although it is also sold powdered for use in the bakery trade and other forms of cooking. Some authorities, however, believe that the cinnamon of the Bible may have been obtained not from *C. zeylanicum* but from *C. cassia*, brought overland from China.

Many fragrant spices known to the Egyptians and later to the Greeks and Romans reached the West by camel and donkey trains belonging to early spice traders.

Muhammad (AD 570–632), founder of Islam, was in early life a spice merchant and the part owner of a business in Mecca trading in myrrh, frankincense, and Oriental spices. Early followers of Islam emulated him, becoming experts not only in the perfume trade but also in discovering scientific methods of extracting flower scents and in distilling essential oils from aromatic plants. Fragrant odours were – and still are – important to Muslims, as is illustrated by their legend that when Muhammad was taken up to heaven some of his sweat fell to earth and from it sprang the rose. 'Who smells the scent of the rose, smells Muhammad.'

Although there is less direct evidence of the use of herbs in the Orient, it is believed by some authorities that they were recognized and used in China for their curative properties from around 2700 BC. This is the time when the emperor Shen Nung, according to legend the founder of Chinese medicine, is reputed to have written his *Pen T'sao Ching* or Herbal, which catalogues more than a hundred herbs and gives prescriptions for their use. Modern Chinese scholars, however, have questioned this date, arguing that, since no written language existed in Shen Nung's time, the Herbal must have been written much later. They suggest that it was compiled, by several authors, in the 1st century AD. This means that certainly by this time the Chinese were using herbs and Frederic Rosengarten in *The Book of Spices* reports a reliable tradition that Chinese courtiers of the 3rd century BC were forced to hold cloves in their mouths as breath sweeteners when addressing their emperor.

Gradually a two-way traffic between East and West spread knowledge of fragrant plants and their products. Vast quantities of perfumes and aromatics were used in Assyria, in Babylonia (where herbs were harvested and prepared by moonlight in the belief that this enhanced their powers), and in Persia (where the surgeon Susruta enumerated more than seven hundred drugs of plant origin and recommended using them to fumigate beds and sickrooms when operations were performed).

The Romans employed spices extravagantly, including adding them to wine and lamp oil. Saffron and rose petals were highly prized, and Nero is said to have used a whole year's supply of cinnamon at the funeral in AD 65 of his wife Poppaea.

Britain acquired scented flowers and plants from two sets of conquerors, first the Romans and later the Normans. The Romans are thought to be responsible for introducing *Rosa gallica officinalis*, the apothecary's rose, so called because its dried petals retain their scent longer than any other rose. They also brought caraway, rosemary, basil, and mint to Britain. It was Norman monks, though, who introduced *Dianthus caryophyllus*, the parent of modern carnations.

RIGHT:
Rosa gallica officinalis, the apothecary's rose, cultivated since time immemorial and the parent of countless hybrids

BELOW:
A very old pink, known in the 14th century, which gets its common name of 'sops in wine' from the practice of spicing wine with its flowers

The awareness of scented plants in Britain increased during the Crusades, when many fragrant plants were brought home by soldiers returning from the Holy Lands – among them scented snowdrops, now alas rare; *Crocus sativus*, the source of saffron; *Rosa damascena*, the damask rose; *Lilium candidum*, the madonna lily; and *Iris florentina*, the source of orris.

But interest in the cultivation and use of scented plants during the Middle Ages was maintained and increased chiefly in the monasteries. In those days care of the sick was mostly in the hands of the monks and so medicinal herbs were grown in monastery gardens. Fragrant and culinary herbs were cultivated too, for church decoration and to enliven the monks' simple diet.

As time went by and the influence of the monasteries waned and finally ended when they were abolished under the Tudors, lay householders – fencing their property to prevent damage by animals – started to grow culinary and ornamental plants. The tendency was to create knot gardens – many small beds grouped into intricate designs, each bed being planted with one variety of plant, and bordered with fragrant thymes, box, lavender, or rosemary, kept dwarf by clipping. It was usually the mistress of the house who controlled the use and harvesting of such plants.

Apart from their medicinal and culinary uses, scented flowers and

ABOVE:
An early European herb garden – a source of medicinal, culinary, and fragrant herbs

LEFT:
The beautifully scented flowers of *Iris florentina*, from whose roots orris is produced

aromatic leaves were strewn on pew seats and church and manor floors; fashioned into decorations for statues and shrines; made into garlands on religious and other occasions; burned in order to purify the air, particularly in damp, cold rooms; fashioned into pomanders; scattered among clothes and linen; and used to give colour and flavour to wines and ales.

Then followed a period when there seems to have been less interest in the cultivation of scented plants, possibly because in the 16th and 17th centuries stronger scents were reaching Europe from the Far East, the West Indies, and Mexico. These included ginger, pepper, nutmegs, mace, cinnamon, and cloves – all highly important to mask and make palatable unsavoury meat and other foods, which often had to be kept for long periods without the benefit of refrigeration or other effective means of preservation.

Spain and Portugal, working mainly in the Spice Islands of the Far East, were pioneers of this trade. Much cruelty was involved in the harvesting of spices – the Portuguese enslaved the islanders and inflicted savage punishments when quotas were not met. When, in 1636, the Dutch occupied Ceylon they were just as cruel to their cinnamon slaves as the Portuguese had been. Britain founded the East India Company in 1600 and there was constant fighting with the Dutch, until a treaty of 1824 resulted in agreed divisions of territory. Towards the end of the 18th century the young United States of America joined the spice-trading nations.

LEFT:
'Here's rosemary for remembrance' – *Rosmarinus officinalis*, an evergreen shrub of dense, leafy habit that has been cultivated for centuries

BELOW:
The common box (*Buxus sempervirens*) a useful small-leaved evergreen, popular for hedging and topiary

BELOW LEFT:
'Of lovely, sweet scents' – a 19th-century woodcut by Weiditz

When Queen Victoria came to the throne in Britain there was revived interest in gardening, and with it a renewed interest in the growing of scented plants. Gardening magazines, and books from William Robinson, the Loudons, Shirley Hibberd, and others, stimulated interest; collectors like Robert Fortune and William Lobb went abroad to search for new plants; Joseph Paxton flowered the scented giant water lily *Victoria amazonica*; and fine new gardens were constructed, many with greenhouses to safeguard tender plants. Prince Albert became President of the Royal Horticultural Society in 1858. The queen herself showed signs of horticultural interest — in 1840 she visited a Mrs Lawrence in order to view her night-flowering, sweet-scented cactus.

After Victoria's death, the great Edwardian gardeners William Robinson and Gertrude Jekyll continued to encourage British gardeners to fill their flower beds with scented plants. Today, a garden full of fragrance is more than ever desirable.

Victoria amazonica, the giant water lily from South America, for which Joseph Paxton built at Chatsworth a special new conservatory which became the model for the great glass house he designed for the Exhibition of 1851

THE USES OF
SCENTED PLANTS

Rosmarinus officinalis, rosemary

IN EARLY TIMES scented plants were not only valued for purifying purposes but used in medicines, as food seasoning, and also made into toilet accessories. Some may have been enjoyed as cut flowers and we have some evidence of this in the fact that Cleopatra is reputed to have had rose petals, several inches deep, spread on the palace floors when entertaining Mark Antony.

We know too that the ancient Greeks and Romans strewed rose petals and fragrant leaves on seats where people congregated to witness games, plays, or fights. The Greeks were more circumspect in their use than the Romans, who went to extravagant lengths with roses particularly, even forcing them out of season with the aid of hot water to ensure constant supplies. Wealthy Romans after bathing would powder their bodies with dried, fragrant rose petals then anoint themselves with oil of roses.

A Roman lady at her toilet (Courtesy the Mary Evans Picture Library)

Nero apparently spent huge sums on roses for banquets, while the Emperor Elagabalus, who reigned AD 218–222 and became noteworthy for 'incredible folly, superstition and vice', is recorded as having had so many roses dropped through apertures in the ceiling at one banquet that several guests were suffocated.

Participants at Roman religious festivals and games frequently wore chaplets of flowers or foliage. Every plant used had a particular meaning. Thus wild flowers and grasses denoted a general responsible for raising the siege of a beleaguered town or city; bay laurel was permitted for victors in war; oak denoted someone with civic virtues; while ivy revealed that the wearer was a poet.

Chaplets of roses were favourite wear for guests at a Roman banquet, which became known as 'the hour when the rose reigns'. This probably accounts for the extravagance of some Roman emperors. After dinner gossip was deemed privileged, and diplomatic

The lush foliage and brilliantly coloured flowers of the scented shrub rose 'Roseraie de l'Hay'

conversations respected, in places where a rose hung from the ceiling or the participants wore rose wreaths on their heads. From this association the term 'sub rosa' or 'under the rose' came in the course of time to mean 'in secret' or 'in confidence'.

But there were other uses for fragrant flowers and leaves. Citizens of the Greek town of Sybaris, founded in 720 BC, attained so much wealth that 'Sybarite' became a synonym for a luxury-loving voluptuary. Sybarites reputedly slept on mattresses filled with rose petals. Was this perhaps the origin of the saying 'a bed of roses'?

In medieval Britain floors were strewn with rushes and sweet-smelling herbs. Later, according to Charles I's herbalist, John Parkinson (1567–1650), Elizabeth I was particularly partial to meadowsweet (*Filipendula ulmaria*) for this purpose and 'did more desire it than any other sweet herbe to strew her chambers withal'. Fragrant herbs were sold by apothecaries. Until very recently, British high-court judges carried posies of sweet-smelling herbs in

RIGHT:
Lavender (*Lavendula spica*), white-flowered sneezewort (*Achillea ptarmica* 'The Pearl'), and a shrubby, golden-yellow *Potentilla fruticosa*

BELOW:
Filipendula ulmaria 'Aurea', the variegated-leaved form of meadowsweet, Queen Elizabeth I's favourite strewing herb

memory of the days when such precautions were necessary to mask the smell of unwashed humanity. As late as the 19th century physicians carried on top of their walking sticks a little box filled with aromatic herbs (like rosemary and lavender) and perfumes, which they sniffed from time to time when visiting patients, to protect themselves against infection.

Perfumes as such did not come into general use in Britain until the reign of Elizabeth I, who was particularly fond of wearing perfumed gloves and who usually carried a pomander – a ball of various aromatic substances that, like the doctor's box, was supposed to protect against infection.

The housewife of the period put the products of plants from her garden to a variety of uses. She became an authority on the herbal treatment of minor ills, but she also made possets and cordials, herbal wines, herb soups and puddings, rose and lavender washing balls, and numerous flower-based powders, soaps, and oils.

Parfums de Fleurs – a 19th-century advertisement for perfume (Courtesy the Mary Evans Picture Library)

THE RELEASE
OF SCENTS

Water lily *Nymphaea* 'Blue Beauty'

THE FRAGRANT PART OF A PLANT is not always the flower. Leaves, bark, and even the roots of certain plants yield perfumes, although they may be released only through damage, for example bruising the foliage or puncturing the bark.

There is a general awareness of a mixture of scents when one ventures into the garden at any season of the year. In spring a fine morning reveals a miscellany of perfumes, a general air of freshness suggestive of burgeoning growth and early flowers. Summer brings awareness of stronger smells – the sweetness of roses, the fruity tang of bearded irises, and the richness of lilies produce a blend that is even more distinctive if it also contains the delicious scent of newly mown grass as it turns to hay. Autumn however suggests ripeness, with fruits, herbs, and vegetables combining in a glorious mixture of flavours.

Gardens reveal their scents in a variety of ways. The pleasantest fragrances of all are perhaps those that come unbidden on currents of air. The English philosopher and author Francis Bacon (1561–1626) was one of the earliest writers to list the plants that give off their fragrance in this way, in his essay 'Of Gardens': 'And because the breath of flowers is far sweeter in the Air (where it comes and goes, like the Warbling of Musick) than in the hand, therefore nothing is more fit for that delight, than to know what be the flowers and plants that do best perfume the Air. Roses, Damask and Red, are fast Flowers of their Smells, so that you may walk by a whole row of them, and find nothing of their Sweetness; yea though it be in a morning's Dew. Bays, likewise, yield no Smell as they grow; Rosemary little, nor Sweet Marjoram.'

Bacon augmented these shrewd observations by noting a few other sources of fragrance that he found pleasing – musk roses, dying strawberry leaves, sweet briar, and lime trees. (I wonder how many people today can pick up and appreciate the smell of dying strawberry leaves in the air?) There are, of course, very many others not mentioned by Bacon, some with airborne scents so strong as to be intrusive, particularly if one ventures too close to them, although such symptoms usually disappear when the scents are inhaled at a distance. The phenomenon is most marked in some species of lilies, mock-orange flowers (*Philadelphus*), hyacinths, freesias, and privet, all of which when brought as cut blooms into the house can affect some people with headaches and symptoms of nausea.

A double variety, 'The Pearl', of the heavily perfumed tuberose from Mexico, *Polianthes tuberosa*

Certain tropical plants have almost overpowering scents, for example frangipani (*Plumeria acuminata*), gardenias (*Gardenia jasminoides*), tuberoses (*Polianthes tuberosa*), and a number of wattles (*Acacia* species). Night-blooming plants also have strong scents, possibly because the air is usually stiller than in the daytime. On warm evenings this is particularly marked in plants like the evening primrose (*Oenothera biennis*), honeysuckles (*Lonicera* species), night-scented stock (*Matthiola bicornis*), and tobacco plants (*Nicotiana alata*). In tropical regions the evening air is made fragrant by the marvel of Peru (*Mirabilis jalapa*), by water lilies (*Nymphaea* species), and most strongly of all by the cactus called queen of the night (*Selenicereus grandiflorus*), whose white blooms, heavily marked with golden rays, and 12in (30cm) across, release their scent in puffs at half-hourly intervals.

Yet flower scents are not all things to all men. Their appreciation by individuals is very much a personal matter, which explains why

The Cape jasmine (*Gardenia jasminoides*), a greenhouse shrub with pure white, fragrant flowers, ideal for cutting

The evening primrose (*Oenothera biennis*),
whose scent fills the air on warm summer
evenings

a plant which possesses a pleasant smell for one person proves offensive to another. Some folk believe that dark-haired people have a sharper sense of smell than those with fair hair, and that albinos have no sense of smell at all. I believe however that we all have a blind spot. Although I have a strong sense of smell, for instance, I find that I cannot relate in any way to the scent of wet box leaves (*Buxus sempervirens*), although others find it 'refreshing and delightful'.

There is often a tendency to describe flower scents in terms of familiar foods, perhaps because the olfactory glands are closely linked to the sense of taste. The English horticulturist, writer, and artist E. A. Bowles (1865–1954) had a remarkably strong sense of smell and he taught me a great deal about flower scents. His favourite scented plants were the cowslip and the similarly perfumed yellow-flowered *Clematis rehderiana* – he once said that if 'heaven smelt of anything he was sure it would be of cowslips'. The flower scent of *Staphylea colchica* he likened to the coconut ices he enjoyed as a child, that of *Magnolia stellata* to a beanfield, and that of the early-blooming winter heliotrope (*Petasites fragrans*) to the almond paste on a fruit cake.

I enjoyed also his tart comments about plants whose scent he disliked. Hawthorn, he said, smelled of fish, meadowsweet of curry, and phlox of a combination of pigs and pepper. Strangely, I enjoy the scent of all these flowers, my own *bête noire* being all the tagetes. I abhor the unpleasant odour of these marigolds, and would not willingly cultivate them anywhere in the garden. Other plants I find unpleasant are *Stapelia* species, all the flowers of which smell to me like bad meat; *Cimicifuga foetida*, an autumn-flowering bugbane, and the tree *Cotoneaster frigida*, both of which reek of decayed fish; and *Dracunculus vulgaris*, an arum with chocolate-coloured flowers, which releases a smell of carrion.

Worse still is the hairy arum (*Helicodiceros crinitus*), which I continue to grow out of interest, although its evil appearance and still more appalling smell always upset visitors, who think something has died in the garden. Fortunately it is only in flower for two or three days, during which time it is best viewed at a distance – preferably through a telescope! It has a huge, purple, arum-like flower, which Bowles likened to a sow's ear, with a central hairy inner spike or spadix that resembles a rat's tail. The stench from these blooms is so vile that all the bluebottles of the district rush to the

LEFT:
The night-blooming marvel of Peru (*Mirabilis jalapa*), whose fragrant, trumpet-like flowers may be white, pink, or yellow

BELOW:
The sinister-looking, evil-smelling hairy arum (*Helicodiceros crinitus*)

RIGHT:
A May-flowering shrub, the bladdernut
(*Staphylea colchica*), which flourishes in the
shade and smells like rice pudding

BELOW:
Shrubby geraniums (*Pelargonium* spp.),
grown for their aromatic leaves and here
mixed with various bedding plants

feast, worming their way down through the hairs to the base of the flowers, where they lay their eggs. Being unable to emerge they ultimately die, the maggots starve soon after hatching, and the flower's ovaries fail to function under the rotting mass. So, at least in Britain, satisfaction is denied to all – the insects go to their deaths and the plant fails to reproduce. Obviously, better results are obtained in the plant's native Corsica. Unpleasant-smelling plants like this are best kept well away from the house and sitting-out areas!

The scents derived from bruised leaves are normally pleasant. Most culinary herbs come into this category, as well as trees and shrubs like sweet bay (*Laurus nobilis*), lavender, rosemary, southernwood (*Artemisia abrotanum*), lemon-scented verbena (*Lippia citriodora*), scented geraniums, eucalyptus, and sweet gale or bog myrtle (*Myrica gale*). A number of conifers – such as *Abies balsamea*, *Cupressus sempervirens*, *C. zeylanicum*, *Libocedrus decurrens*, and many of the *Picea* species – also release pleasant scents when their leaves are

A richly scented, day-flowering tropical water lily – *Nymphaea pennsylvania* 'Blue Beauty'

Italian cypress (*Cupressus sempervirens*), much cultivated in medieval Europe for its fragrant, moth-repelling wood

bruised. Other plants may have aromatic rootstocks, particularly the roseroot (*Rhodiola rosea*), a succulent found in stony subalpine situations in the Scottish Highlands, parts of Wales, and the north of Ireland. It has fleshy leaves, yellow flowers, and thick fleshy roots which have a pleasant rose-like odour when freshly broken. The perfume is delicious and is retained in the dried roots for several weeks. The roots of *Iris florentina* have a scent of violets, which becomes more pronounced as they dry and wither; they are powdered and sold as orris root. Another iris, *I. foetidissima*, is often called the roast-beef plant because of the smell of its roots and leaves.

Although we cannot have every form of fragrant plant growing in our gardens, there are enough reliable and hardy kinds to afford us pleasure for most of the year, while some of the others are possibilities for the home and greenhouse.

THE FRAGRANT
GARDEN

Santolina neapolitana, cotton lavender

SCENTED PLANTS can be established in various situations and garden settings. Some gardeners, for example, may be primarily interested in a mixture of scents, and accordingly aim to find fragrance in a variety of situations as they wander through their gardens. Some may be particularly attracted to certain plants, such as roses or lilies, and will grow them to the exclusion of other species. Others, who prefer a continuous season of pleasant scents, will grow a wider range of plants, including some that need touching to release their aromas. Others still may concentrate on plants that can be grown near the house, where they can be enjoyed by those who have to spend a lot of time indoors. They will plant nocturnal bloomers in places where the family congregates on summer evenings.

In an arid country like Spain and the South American lands of Ecuador, Colombia and Venezuela (together known as New Granada at the time of the Spanish Conquest), enclosed patio gardens are often constructed in the centre of the home buildings. These are quite private and a joy to visit, with their emphasis on peace and quiet and their lavish use of green colouring, playing fountains, and sweet scents. I particularly remember a patio garden in Bogota, Colombia, close to the Colonial Museum and nearby crowded streets, which when entered revealed a bower of beauty. Eucalyptus trees, acacias, a *Magnolia grandiflora*, lantanas, daturas, various honeysuckles, and even a rosemary – all of them fragrant and many growing in large terracotta pots – released a plethora of scents, while caged song birds and playing fountains provided a musical background.

Then of course there are herb gardens, a necessity for all good cooks and also a source of material for scents, medicines, and cosmetics.

In medieval times these were essentially kitchen gardens, growing, besides culinary herbs, poisonous plants to use against enemies and magical herbs for love potions. Important since Saxon times, herb gardens in Elizabethan days were symmetrically laid out, the varieties usually kept distinct, but always planted in geometrically shaped beds – round, square, or diamond – edged with box, yew, santolina, or lavender kept short by regular clipping. Remnants of these can sometimes be seen in old gardens in Britain and the United States of America.

Today herbs are often grouped together, rather less formally, to

RIGHT:
A summer border, with roses, campion (*Lychnis chalcedonica*), salvias, campanulas, and hardy *Geranium endressii* at Pusey House in Wiltshire

PAGES 40–41
LEFT:
A scented border at Waterperry, Oxford, with madonna lilies, antirrhinums, and clary sage (*Salvia sclarea*)

ABOVE RIGHT:
A garden of fragrance at Newby Hall, Ripon

BELOW RIGHT:
The Royal Horticultural Society's scented garden at Wisley in Surrey

make a separate garden feature where their scents and subtle differences of leaf shapes, colours, and textures can be more readily appreciated. Given the opportunity when making such a feature, choose an open sunny position, since this will suit a greater range of herbs and their fragrance will be more marked. The effects of sunlight will also enhance their flavour for culinary purposes, and if the bed is within easy reach of the kitchen this could be an asset. Some low-growing decorative herbs, such as variegated sages and thymes, make interesting border edgings for flower as well as herb beds, while the taller kinds – especially angelica (which is particularly handsome in bloom), lavenders, rosemary, and cotton lavender (*Santolina* species) – are often grown with other, purely decorative, flowers in mixed borders or even used as accent plants in key positions in the main garden.

However, one must not overlook a tendency to spreading by certain herbs. Mints, for example, are particularly prone to this fault and difficult to eradicate when really well established. The solution is to confine the roots, either by growing them in a bottomless metal container, such as an old pail, pushing this down into the soil so that the rim is just hidden, or by driving metal strips down in the same way to form a confined area. Another idea is to make a bed in the shape of a wheel – the spokes becoming paths if constructed of narrow strips of stone, wood, or bricks. Push slates or thick sheets of plastic perpendicularly down into the soil each side of the spokes, and plant a different kind of herb in each section. If plants with coloured foliage and with various flower shapes are included the herb garden will be visually attractive for most of the year.

Other ideas and shapes may suggest themselves, such as open-work 'baskets' of various patterns as well as paths made not of stone, but using plants of prostrate habit that do not resent being trodden on. The peppermint scented *Mentha requienii*, chamomile, and sundry small thymes are all suitable, as is *Calamintha acinus*, which releases a minty smell when walked on. All of these will retain their foliage throughout the year.

Low-growing herbs and scented plants can also be used to break up flat expanses of paving, if spaces are left between the slabs and the resulting soil pockets dug over and fertilized before planting.

Herbs are undemanding in their soil requirements. Given the choice, however, one should make herb gardens in well-drained, fertile soil and in an open position, possibly consigning those, like

LEFT:
The herb border and a corner of the knot garden at Barnsley House, Gloucestershire

BELOW:
One of the prettiest of old-fashioned herbs, *Calamintha nepeta*, which has a mint-like aroma

mint, that will tolerate wetter and shadier conditions to a less favourable spot.

Although often consigned to the vegetable area, herbs can make an effective ornamental feature. Herbal colour combinations can be most attractive. Soft grey-green or silver foliage may be interspersed with touches of blue provided by lavender, sage, chive flowers, and catmint or with pinks and reds provided by bergamots, coloured primroses, and garden pinks. A gold or a white garden is another possibility, for many herbs have variegated or coloured foliage and there are plenty of fragrant perennials and annuals to grow between.

Suggestions for a border of pleasingly scented flowers – not necessarily herbs – are given on pages 94–6. Such a border *must* be planned on paper before planting – it is much easier to pencil in a different plant on a plan than later have to dig up something that looks totally out of place in the garden.

Scented plants can be grown in window boxes or containers, in the home and greenhouse as well as in the garden. There is no limit to the possibilities, some of which are discussed on page 98.

Many herbs and scented plants are best used when fresh – flowers intended for bouquets, buttonholes, and corsage sprays, for example, as well as herbs for sauces and flavourings. But herbs can also be dried in order to enhance the taste of winter meals, or used for aromatic purposes such as making into pomanders, scent sachets, and pot-pourri.

However, careful preparation and drying is essential. It is more difficult to harvest and dry plants successfully than to grow them. Timing is all-important – the plants should be gathered at their peak and in dry, sunny weather. It is no accident that most commercially cultivated spices and scent plants are grown in countries that have warm climates.

Damp, dull days defeat crisp drying. Leaves become limp if they reabsorb moisture, turning mildewy and musty, and once this happens they lose their desirable qualities. Outdoor drying in a warm current of air is the ideal, with the plants hung upside down in small bunches. In cool climates this may be difficult, so they are frequently dried in racks or on trays indoors, in a light airy room. In every case the drying area should be away from direct sunlight, which dries out the tissues too quickly with the loss of much of the scent. Similarly, neither fragrant flowers, culinary herbs, nor

Cotton lavender (*Santolina neapolitana*), an evergreen shrub with fragrant silver leaves and golden flowers

scented foliage should be cut when wet or even damp – wait until dew or mist has dispersed or been dried off by warm winds or sun. When gathering flowers intended for pot-pourri and scent bags, remove the flowers from the stems – or just the petals in the case of large blooms like roses – and spread them out on trays, turning them daily to hasten the drying. Once this is completed put the dried blooms in airtight containers, sealing them securely to retain the scent until the flowers are needed. Wooden or pottery containers are better than tins or plastic boxes.

Plants liable to shed their florets during drying – such as lavender – should be gathered before they are fully out and dried on trays or racks with paper or boxes underneath to catch the blooms as they fall. Alternatively, hang them upside down in small bunches, enclosing the flower heads in paper bags. Similarly, when harvesting plants grown for their aromatic seeds – such as caraway, coriander, sesame, cumin, and dill – the seed heads should be removed only when they are quite dry. They can then be dropped in a cardboard box and removed to a dry room. Now place the heads in thin muslin bags and hang them up to complete the drying process, after which the seeds can be separated from the pods and stored in the airtight jars that will be their more permanent homes.

A selection of aromatic plants and herbs for drying

SPRING

FRESHNESS

Convallaria majalis 'Variegata', lily of the valley

THE LONGEST and severest of winters eventually comes to a close. Spring arrives, bringing a medley of scents released by a few early flowers to give promise of joys to come. As the days pass, rain and sunshine swell the buds of later blooms and finally spring eases into summer with a riotous display of blossom.

Spring is also a time to attend to gardening tasks, including tidying lawns and flower beds, removing winter-damaged tree branches, and preparing the ground for seed sowing. It is also a good time for planting new shrubs and herbaceous perennials.

Because scent as well as blossom is now more in evidence there is no need to relegate aromatic plants to a specific area as one might in winter, when they are frequently kept near to the house, so that they can be easily seen and smelled. It is pleasant to be led from one scent to another during a spring walk, so shrubs and trees can be interspersed, and in some cases underplanted, with fragrant spring bulbs, now both plentiful and varied.

In early spring some of the most spectacular trees for the garden are magnolias. They are of very ancient lineage; fossil remains dating back five million years are common over wide areas of northeast America and east Asia. With a careful choice of hardy varieties flowering can be extended over a period of several months. Among spring-blooming deciduous trees few are easier to establish than a hybrid from the fragrant Chinese *Magnolia denudata* called *M. × soulangiana*. This grows into a 10–15 ft (3–4.5 m) high, spreading, rather more shapely tree than its parent. It produces hundreds of chalice-shaped flowers, each 5–6 in (13–15 cm) across, in April; the flowers are white with purple-stained bases. There are a number of varieties, mainly differing in the degree of purple in the flowers. All are fragrant, but a particularly fine variety is 'Lennei', which is rose-purple outside and white within and which often bears a second crop of blooms in the autumn.

More suitable for small gardens, however, as it will flower when quite tiny (from 1 ft, 30 cm), is the deciduous Japanese *M. stellata*. Given a sheltered situation, protected from buffeting east winds, the white, starry, fragrant, 3–4 in (8–10 cm) blooms come early, to be followed by lemon-scented, lance-shaped leaves. The bark too has a pleasant scent. Plenty of moist peat should be worked into the soil to encourage growth, which should result after some years in a shrub 8–10 ft (2.5–3 m) high. Try underplanting *M. stellata* with

The early-flowering *Magnolia stellata*, which has lemon-scented buds and leaves as well as fragrant blossoms

blue grape hyacinths (*Muscari armeniacum*), as the two bloom at the same time.

Alice Coats, in *Garden Flowers and their Histories*, says that, given time, even small magnolias 'seem destined to grow to a size proportionable to their large and noble flowers'. However this has not been my experience with *M. stellata*, which in our garden is still only 4½ ft (1.4 m) high after more than twelve years. It is now considered to be a dwarf sport or mutant of *M. kobus*, and a shrub highly suitable for most gardens, large or small.

Although too large to plant in many gardens there are hedgerows, woodland areas, and open fields where the odd tall tree is welcome, particularly if it has an unusual gift to bestow.

Three North American poplars fulfil this requisite – *Populus balsamifera*, the balsam poplar; *P. trichocarpa*, the black cottonwood; and *P. candicans*, often but erroneously known as Balm of Gilead (the true Balm of Gilead is the thorny *Commiphora opobalsam*). All these deciduous poplars have their winter buds thickly coated with sticky, yellow, very fragrant resin, which discharges an almost overpowering scent of balsam when the buds open in spring to release their long, pointed leaves.

Although many tree fruits flower in spring, including a host of ornamental cherries, few except apples are noted for scent. The few other exceptions include the Yoshino Cherry (*Prunus* × *yedoensis*), which although widely cultivated in Japan is apparently unknown in the wild. This has great quantities of slightly fragrant white blossoms in March and early April. A white Japanese hybrid called 'Jonior' produces a scent reminiscent of gorse. Others worth noting are *Prunus padus*, the bird cherry, which carries its white, almond-scented flowers in slender, drooping racemes in May, along with the leaves, and *P. subhirtella* 'Pendula', a lovely, slender, weeping tree of medium size, very slightly fragrant, with pink or white blossoms in March and April.

The European gorse (*Ulex europaeus*), also known as whin or furze, is abundant in the British Isles, frequently covering large areas of rough ground, including whole hillsides and steep roadside banks, with its intricate branches and formidable shiny leaves. Yet it is by no means widespread elsewhere, even in Europe. Sir James E. Smith (1759–1828), in his *English Botany*, writes that Linnaeus, the great Swedish botanist, who visited England in 1736, fell to his knees on Putney Heath in amazement and thanksgiving when he saw the gorse growing there. Curiously, the same story is told about other great botanists at other places and other times, including Dillenius at Hounslow Heath in 1721 and Peter Kalm at Fulham Common in 1745. However, we know that Linnaeus experienced great difficulties in getting the plant to grow in Sweden, even in a greenhouse.

Another admirer of gorse was the great plant collector Frank Kingdon Ward (1885–1958), who once said that gorse was the outstanding plant he would have chosen to bring to Britain had it not already been a native.

Gorse starts to flower in February, becomes a brilliant mass of gold around April and May, and goes on producing stray blooms throughout the year. However, and not withstanding the rich scent of the golden, pea-shaped flowers, few will seek to grow this untidy shrub in the garden. The double-flowered form 'Flore Pleno' is not only smaller and more compact, but superior in every way, with scent something like that of laburnum. It needs a sunny position in poor dryish soil, thus making it a good subject for a rough bank as well as a formidable deterrent to intruders. As this form does not produce seed it has to be propagated in August from 3–4 in (7.5–10 cm) cuttings of the current season's growth, rooted in a peat and sand mixture in a cold frame.

Among smaller shrubs, the deciduous *Fothergilla gardenii* from the

The fragrant stamens of the petal-less witch alder (*Fothergilla gardenii*)

United States grows a mere 2–3 ft (60–90 cm) in height, with spreading branches supporting young twigs covered with white hair and oval leaves with heart-shaped bases. The scented flowers – all petal-less but with showy white and yellow stamens – appear before the foliage in April, borne on rounded terminal branches. *F. major* grows taller (6–10 ft, 1.8–3 m) and has numerous pinkish-white scented blossoms. Added attractions are the vivid red, orange, and yellow foliage tints that appear prior to leaf-fall.

Viburnum farreri and *V. × bodnantense* are often still in flower in April, when they are joined by the most highly fragrant member of the genus. This is *V. carlesii*, long popular as a deciduous garden shrub, which is unrivalled for scent. Given deep loamy soil and a sheltered position, protected from north and east winds, and from early morning sun liable to damage frosted buds, it is not difficult to grow. Moisture is essential however, which is why it sometimes fails in shallow, hungry soils. The species grows 5–8 ft (1.5–2.5 m) high and has roughly ovate leaves and rounded 2–3 in (5–8 cm) heads of waxy-white, powerfully fragrant flowers. It is the parent of some widely grown hybrids, including *V. × carlcephalum*, which has larger leaves and in May flowers in dense 6 in (15 cm) trusses, pink in the bud opening to white with a pink flush. This form grows to 8 ft (2.5 m), but in spite of its larger flower trusses it lacks the elegance of its parent.

Other *V. carlesii* derivatives include *V. × burkwoodii*, an 8 ft (2.5 m) shrub which thrives in most soils. The flowers, which are pinkish when young but develop to white, are carried in fragrant, rounded 2–3 in (5–8 cm) clusters. It is also nearly evergreen, totally so in a mild winter. *V.* 'Anne Russell' has still finer pink-budded flowers in 3 in (8 cm) clusters. *V. × juddii* is a free-flowering form, the blooms not quite so sweetly scented, but making a plant of 5 ft (1.5 m) with a strong constitution.

All these viburnums may be propagated from cuttings – softwood in summer, rooted over bottom heat; heel cuttings in sand and peat in June and July. Alternatively, they may be layered in early autumn without much difficulty.

Other early shrubs with varying degrees of attraction and scent include the flowering currant *Ribes sanguineum*, whose trusses of scarlet flowers and rich-smelling palmate leaves remind some people of blackcurrants, but others of cats. The bushes bloom freely and readily in most gardens, and also open from bud when cut

Flower clusters of *Viburnum × burkwoodii*, pride of the spring garden

branches are brought indoors. The yellow-flowered *R. odoratum* is clove-scented.

Several tall heathers start to flower in April and May, or even earlier in a mild season. Since these come from north Africa or southern Europe they are not reliably hardy. *Erica arborea*, the tree heath of north Africa, although it attains a height of more than 20 ft (6 m) in the wild, is unlikely to reach more than 8 ft (2.5 m) or 10 ft (3 m) in the garden. The hardiest form is 'Alpina', which is a hand-some evergreen with fresh-looking foliage and stiff pyramids of white, honey-scented flowers. Another fragrant variety is *E. erigena* 'Superba'. It makes a bushy, very hardy plant of 6–8 ft (1.8–2.5 m), with an abundance of rich, rosy red flowers from March to May.

Osmanthus delavayi, described by the British nurseryman Sir Harold Hillier (1905–85) as 'one of China's gems', is a beautiful evergreen, 4–6 ft (1.2–1.8 m) tall, with small, stiff, leathery leaves and sweetly scented white, jessamine-like flowers borne in profu-

Osmanthus delavayi, with its beautiful jessamine-like flowers – 'one of the best white-flowered evergreens of spring'

sion in April. It is one of the best white-flowered evergreens of spring, with a fragrance to match its overall charm. It can be propagated from cuttings taken in July and rooted with bottom heat. Another species, *O. heterophyllus* is noteworthy because of the resemblance of its leaves to those of holly, but its small, white, scented flowers are inconspicuous and do not appear until autumn.

For those with the right conditions a tree which cannot fail to give pleasure in spring is the Australian wattle (*Acacia dealbata*). It needs both warmth and sunlight and the protection of a warm wall or at least shelter from icy winds. Good plants, though, can be grown in large pots or soil borders in greenhouses or sun lounges, provided the temperature never falls below 39° F (4° C). Plenty of light is also necessary to ripen the wood and guarantee flowering the following spring. Under good conditions this acacia will grow to 20 ft (6 m), although growth can be restricted by careful pruning. The silvery, finely cut, fern-like leaves grow on long slender stems, and have fluffy, bright golden clusters of ball-like flowers. These are petal-less and powerfully fragrant. Although they do not remain fluffy when removed from the tree, cut sprays are sent to Britain in spring from southern Europe in large quantities, under the name of mimosa. The species should be grown in good soil compost and fed at fortnightly intervals between May and October. Propagation can be effected by means of heel cuttings rooted in a warm propagating frame in summer. Another species often grown in pots is *A. armata*, the kangaroo thorn. An evergreen, it rarely exceeds 10 ft (3 m) in height but makes a dense bush with very thorny leaves and fragrant, rich golden flowers all along the stems. Less heat is needed for this species than for *A. dealbata*.

Some years ago in Virginia I saw a formidable boy- and dog-proof hedge made from clipped *Poncirus trifoliata* (*Aegle sepiaria*) bushes. This is the Chinese hardy orange, a deciduous species with green, angular branches well furnished with barbaric, stiff, 1–2 in (2.5–5 cm) pointed thorns. In spring, when the pure white orange-blossom-like flowers appear, their scent is most marked. In some seasons they go on to produce small round orange-like fruits. These are not tasty, although E. A. Bowles sometimes grated the fruits for flavouring purposes and they may be used instead of lemon in China tea. The hardy orange grows to 10 ft (3 m) and needs a sheltered sunny position and deep soil. It never makes a very leafy plant; the stems must take on some of the foliage functions.

The golden flowers of the kangaroo thorn (*Acacia armata*)

The rhododendron group is an enormous one, with at least five hundred species and thousands of cultivars. Many are scented, and the best way to select for colours, types, and fragrance is to visit a specialist nursery when the plants are in bloom and make an 'on the spot' decision. The large evergreen kinds do, however, need a great deal of room, doing best in woodland conditions. Many are sensitive to cold winds and spring frosts and, being members of the heather family, most will not thrive in limy soils.

However, the smaller-growing hybrid azaleas are popular shrubs for small gardens on account of their rich colours, brilliant autumnal tints (in the deciduous kinds), and the almost overpowering rich scent of many cultivars. Most of the hardy hybrids will tolerate sun provided the roots are kept moist with mulches of peat, rotted manure, or compost, but as a general rule all those that flower before the end of May must be planted where they are protected from early morning sun. A sudden thaw following frost will blacken both flowers and buds.

Not all deciduous hybrid azaleas are fragrant, so either make a selection from flowering plants, or study catalogue lists of Ghent hybrids, which grow 4–8 ft (1.2–2.5 m) high and have long-tubed,

RIGHT:
Ghent azaleas, rich in scent and colour

BELOW:
The green stems and formidable thorns of the hardy orange (*Poncirus trifoliata*)

honeysuckle-like flowers with scent to match; of Occidentale hybrids, mostly in soft pastel shades; or of the Rustica hybrids, which have double flowers and bloom later than the others, in late May or early June. The Rusticas will tolerate a more open position. All shades of pink, red, orange, and yellow are represented, some with spots or frilled petal edges, and many exhibit rich autumn colours.

Regular pruning is not necessary with azaleas, although spindly plants can be lightly cut back to make them bushy. If a plant gets too big for its position it is wiser to move it than to cut deeply into the branches. This is quite easy because the root system is very close and compact and easy to lift. The best time for this operation is between September and April, in good weather.

There will naturally also be spill-overs of fragrance from some of the winter shrubs, particularly the mahonias, shrubby honeysuckles, and sarcococcas. The species *Camellia sasanqua* with single, sweetly scented, white flowers, and pleasantly fragrant, glossy dark green leaves, is welcome among so many scentless camellias.

The early foliage of *Rosa primula* has a strong scent of incense, especially after a shower; the small yellow flowers are also fragrant.

Choisya ternata, the Mexican orange blossom, is a useful evergreen shrub for sun or shade, with white, sweetly scented flowers throughout late spring and early summer, plus odd blooms all through the year. The shiny, dark green, trifoliate leaves are also aromatic when crushed and, cut, last a long time indoors. A form with golden leaves called 'Sundance' retains its colouring throughout the year but needs a more sheltered position than the type.

Finally, the European dogwood, *Cornus mas*, flowers in February. This deciduous large shrub or small tree is then studded with small, fragrant, yellow flowers on the naked branches. These are succeeded by small, edible, cherry-like red fruits, known as cornelian cherries. In times of plague, these, because of their supposed antiseptic qualities, were sometimes the only fruits permitted for sale. The fine-grained wood is not easily splintered, so was often used for making into meat skewers. The name 'dogwood' refers to another one-time use of this long-cultivated shrub – its bark was an ingredient in a shampoo for washing mangy dogs.

Spring fragrance may also be derived from a miscellany of bulbs and other soft-stemmed plants. Most gardeners appreciate the rich but heavy scent of hyacinths and the subtler fragrance emitted by

RIGHT:
The long-flowering, scented Mexican orange (*Choisya ternata*), whose leaves also are aromatic when crushed

PAGES 60–61
ABOVE LEFT:
The cornelian cherry (*Cornus mas*), once grown for its edible fruits

BELOW LEFT:
A delight of spring flowers – snowdrops, hellebores, and the honeysuckle *Lonicera fragrantissima*

ABOVE RIGHT:
A beautiful, richly scented, hybrid Dutch hyacinth, 'L'Innocence'

BELOW RIGHT:
The feather, or tassel, hyacinth (*Muscari comosum* 'Plumosum')

several early crocuses, particularly *Crocus laevigatus* and *C. imperati*, both of which are ideal for rock-garden pockets or for cold-greenhouse culture. Then there are snowdrops, *Galanthus* species, whose appeal lies perhaps mainly in their pure white flowers, but which are appreciated also for their scent. Certainly freshly picked snowdrops brought into a warm room have a honey fragrance. E. A. Bowles, in an article in F. C. Stern's book *Snowdrops and Snowflakes*, describes the scent of double snowdrops as a fragrance resembling 'that of a field of buckwheat rather than the heavier heather scent of *G. caucasicus* and *G. alleni*'s imitation of almond blossom'.

Leucojum vernum, the spring snowflake from central Europe, flowers at the same time as the snowdrop, its drooping white flowers being somewhat similar except that all its petal segments are the same length – not short and long as in *Galanthus*. It has a sweet scent resembling that of violets.

Most narcissi have scented flowers, particularly marked in the bunch-flowered *Narcissus jonquilla* group and the Tazettas, which include varieties suitable for growing hydroponically such as 'Paper White', 'Cragford', and 'Geranium'. I am also fond of the small and graceful Triandrus group, which grow only 6–12 in (15–30 cm) high with up to six pendulous, cream, white, or gold flowers on each stem. All are ideal for rock pockets or for growing in pots in a cold greenhouse and all are easily raised from seed. A pretty white variety, 'Angel's Tears', is reputed to have been named for Angelo, a Spanish guide who was hired by the eminent British bulb grower Peter Barr. One day, after climbing the mountains of northwest Spain for a long time looking for plants, Angelo collapsed with strain and tiredness and burst into tears – at which moment he spotted this charming little variety. The season ends with *N. poeticus*, the poet's narcissus, with erect, white, shallow-cupped, richly scented flowers, borne one to a stem, that do not open until May or June.

Other bulbs and corms with scented blooms include bluebells (the Spanish species *Endymion hispanicum* has larger flowers than the English *E. non-scriptus*); *Iris reticulata*, deep blue with a scent of violets; and the grape hyacinths, *Muscari armeniacum*, which is musky scented, and *M. plumosum*, which is more like ripe plums.

The crown imperial, *Fritillaria imperialis*, is the tallest spring-flowering bulb, growing to 4 ft (1.2 m). Each flower stem carries a

'Paper White', one of the heavily aromatic Tazetta narcissi

whorl of pendent, bell-shaped, orange or yellow flowers, surmounted by a bushy topknot of narrow leaves after the fashion of a pineapple fruit. Individual flowers are about $2\frac{1}{2}$ in (6 cm) deep and almost as much across, with six perianth segments and six pearl-like liquid nectaries at the base of each. This nectar is not easily dislodged, even with vigorous shaking, and if dried with blotting paper is replaced within an hour. A charming legend relates how the crown imperial's flowers were once white and looked upwards. It was a very haughty plant through pride in its crown of leaves and in the Garden of Gethsemane, as Jesus passed through, it was the only flower not to bow its head in humility. Gently Jesus rebuked it – at which it hung its head and blushed with shame and tears came into its eyes.

Depicted in many Dutch flower paintings, the crown imperial has been grown in British gardens since the 16th century. At that time there were apparently double varieties as well as silver and

A group of crown imperials (*Fritillaria imperialis*), standing soldierly erect

gold variegated forms. I have solitary plants of the last, but have yet to meet anyone who has seen double-flowered kinds. The large bulbs should be planted 6 in (15 cm) deep in well-drained but good soil and propagated by breaking off portions of the old bulb scales, rooting these in a cold frame. The scent from crown imperials is fleeting, coming across the garden without warning. It is a foxy smell, which I rather like but most people do not. E. A. Bowles once described it as 'a mixture of mangy fox, dirty dog kennel, the small cat's house at the zoo and Exeter railway station'.

Convallaria majalis, the lily of the valley, is the national flower of Finland. It spreads rapidly by means of creeping rootstocks. The long, stalked leaves grow in pairs and the slender, arched stems each support five to eight pendent little white bell-shaped flowers which are richly scented. Lilies of the valley will grow in most soils, either in sun or shade, preferably somewhere between the two. They can be invasive; I find the pink form 'Rosea' a real nuisance between

Three varieties of lily of the valley (*Convallaria majalis*), looking thoroughly at home in a wild garden

shrubs, and the large-flowered 'Fortin's Giant' is another strong grower. Other varieties include 'Prolificans' of which there are two forms – one bearing rows of double flowers along each stem, the other carrying them in groups like miniature bunches of grapes. There are also two with variegated foliage – 'Variegata', which has longitudinal soft yellow stripes, and 'Hardwick Hall', whose broad leaves are outlined with pale gold.

Lily-of-the-valley flowers are always popular for weddings, but in medieval times they were chiefly valued as the source of lily-of-the-valley water, which was credited with strange properties. The herbalist John Gerard (1545–1612) wrote that the liquid, distilled and drunk with wine, 'restores speech unto those that have the dumb palsie, and that are falne into the Apoplexie and comfort the heart'. He also credited it with strengthening the memory and helping eye inflammation. In continental Europe at that time lily-of-the-valley water was called aqua aurea, and was so precious and costly that it was invariably carried in small vessels or lockets of gold and silver.

A few other much-loved, early-flowering and pleasantly scented plants are polyanthus, primroses, cowslips, pansies, and wallflowers, all of which are readily raised from seed. The primrose (*Primula vulgaris*), once widespread in Britain, was eaten in puddings and used to make primrose pottage and primrose vinegar. Today, crystallized primrose flowers are sometimes used for cake decorations, along with violets and rose petals.

The cowslip (*P. veris*) shares the fresh and delicate fragrance of the primrose. Its name is said to have been derived from the resemblance of its scent to the sweet breath of a cow. The roots also have a scent like aniseed.

It is uncertain when the wallflower (*Cheiranthus cheiri*) reached Britain, although most authorities believe it was at the time of the Norman Conquest. Certainly wallflowers were much loved by our ancestors on account of their sweet scent which, according to John Parkinson 'causeth them to be generally used in Nosegayes and to deck up houses'. He himself grew six varieties, including three doubles. One very old variety has survived – a miniature double yellow called 'Harpur Crewe' that Parkinson probably knew. This was rescued from oblivion and propagated at the end of the 19th century by an English clergyman. A good perennial and richly scented, it is propagated from cuttings, not seed. Today wallflowers

The striped leaves and pure white flowers of the lily of the valley 'Variegata'

are obtainable in a wide range of colours and blending of shades, and are suitable for all well-drained soils, including chalk. The seed should be sown soon after harvesting, and when the seedlings are transplanted the point of the tap root should be broken off to encourage fibrous root formation.

The sweet violet (*Viola odorata*) is a British plant that has probably been grown as long as gardens have been cultivated. The flowers were commonly eaten as food sweeteners in the days before sugar was introduced. In the Middle Ages they were also esteemed as a preventative, or cure, for all sorts of pulmonary complaints. Today the flowers are candied for cake decoration. Napoleon I was very fond of violets, which he said reminded him of the Corsican woods where he played as a child, and so, too, was Josephine. When she died, in 1814, Napoleon had violets planted on her grave. After his death some flowers from the grave, crushed, were found in a locket he had always worn around his neck.

The humble sweet violet (*Viola odorata*), beloved of the Romantic poets, the Victorians, and Napoleon

SUMMER'S BOUNTY

Dianthus barbatus, sweet william

UMMER SYMBOLIZES the fulfillment of the gardener's year, when the results of earlier labours come to fruition. It is a season of roses, of rich red paeonies and rainbow irises, of murmuring bees and dripping waterfalls, of new-mown hay and the heady scent of mock orange. Altogether a beautiful time of year, with gardens a riot of colour, and as fast as one flower passes from bloom another takes its place.

The warm summer nights too have a spell-binding beauty. There is temptation to linger outdoors longer than usual, and when the mantle of evening drives all but the very young inside, doors and windows may be left wide open to the still, warm air. If only for this reason we should always grow a few fragrant plants close to the house, so that we can enjoy their scents borne on the evening air. Some of these will be naturally nocturnal, like the night-scented stocks, evening primroses, and, in some settings, tropical water lilies; while tobacco plants and honeysuckles are either more strongly scented after dusk or else practically scentless during the day. The reasons for this must be linked with pollination; scent being a lure to attract insect agents like bees in the daytime or long-tongued moths at night.

Again, the amount of scent emitted may also be linked with growing conditions. Aromatic herbs and plants grown in a warm sheltered position on a dryish soil enjoy a maximum of heat and their scent is noticeably improved. A small, enclosed courtyard may accordingly make a better site for an evening garden than one that is open all round.

Fragrant day blooms in white or pastel shades also show up better in the gloaming than dark reds and purples, so that *Lilium regale*, pale roses, paeonies, and stocks can be planted farther back yet still become obvious to the eye as well as nose.

A major task early in the season is planting bedding material or filling gaps in perennial borders for mid-summer display. The appearance of the garden during the coming months, when it is likely to be well used, is highly important. Assuming that the ground has been cleaned and manured, and that all risk of frost is past, the best time for planting is in showery weather, for then plant roots rapidly take hold and there is little check to growth. If this is not possible, and the ground is dry, water it well a day or so beforehand; and if transplanting from pots soak any that seem dry for an hour beforehand, then turn out and plant the contents without damaging their

A golden-leafed form – *Philadelphus coronarius* 'Aureus' – of the mock orange

soil balls. Use a trowel for making the holes and, after inserting the plants, exert very gentle pressure with both hands to settle them snugly in place.

When bedding plants are bought, check each one carefully. A lot of flowers or buds already on plants is *not* an indication of quality – often the reverse. Select stocky material with clean, bright green leaves. Yellowing leaves, spindly growth, or a stunted habit are points to recognize and avoid.

Even in summer there are flowering trees, some spilling over from spring. Among the hawthorns (*Crataegus* species) are trees much favoured in the past as maypoles on account of the purity of their small white fragrant flowers. The most popular was *C. monogyna*, now usually relegated to hedging, for it tolerates severe and regular cutting, often going under the name 'quick' or 'may'. Crossed with the larger-flowered *C. oxyacantha*, its hybrids are popular as small trees for gardens, especially the pink and red

RIGHT:
The best double-flowered red form of hawthorn – *Crataegus oxyacantha* 'Paul's Scarlet'

BELOW:
Lilium regale, a hardy lily with a rich honeysuckle perfume

single and double forms. These are scented, but to my mind it is an unpleasant, fishy odour.

Later we get the common horse chestnuts (*Aesculus hippocastanum*), with their magnificent slightly honey-scented inflorescences, rising like stiff candles at the tips of the leafy branches. The individual, red-blotched, pure white flowers cannot fail to delight the eye, even if too far away to be smelled.

Limes make their beautiful presence felt when they come to flower in July – although perhaps few people have the room to plant such large trees. *Tilia petiolaris* is particularly fragrant, especially in the evening. Australian eucalyptus trees are increasingly being planted now that hardier varieties have been introduced. Even when cut back in a hard winter they usually break again from the base, due to an ability to form lignotubers – reservoirs of dormant buds at ground level. These enable the trees to sprout fresh growths after a forest fire as well as regenerate new shoots following a bad winter. The silvery evergreen leaves, which are beautiful at all seasons, release a balsamic odour when bruised.

The common elder (*Sambucus nigra*) is rarely planted in gardens, although its golden-foliaged cultivar 'Aurea', the yellow-margined 'Aurea-variegata', and 'Laciniata', with finely cut, fern-like leaves, are frequently introduced in mixed shrubberies. Nevertheless the common native has an ability to grow in rough corners where few other plants could survive, and its flat heads of white flowers in June are wonderfully fragrant. When I was a child elderflowers were infused in boiling water, then the liquid used for hair rinses and as a cooling lotion for the face and eyes. The round, shiny black berries have culinary and medicinal properties.

More garden-worthy than any of these for restricted areas is the small evergreen *Skimmia japonica*. A mere 3–4 ft (90–120 cm) high, compact growing, and equally at home on chalk or acid soils, it should be planted in shade, preferably close to the house as it is worth looking at all through the year. However two plants will be needed, for male and female flowers are borne on separate bushes, and both are necessary for the production of the crowded bunches of scarlet, holly-like fruits. For some reason these are ignored by birds and usually remain on the branches until new flowers appear the following year. Both male and female flowers are white, the male with an almost overpowering lily-of-the-valley scent. There is also a white-berried form and a bisexual species called *S. reevesiana*.

ABOVE RIGHT:
Sambucus nigra 'Aurea' – a gold-foliaged cultivar of the European elder

BELOW RIGHT:
Two species of skimmia growing side by side – *Skimmia japonica* (left) and *S. reevesiana*

Syringa is the family name of lilac, although often wrongly applied to the mock orange, which is actually *Philadelphus*. This name muddle apparently occurred because both plants arrived in Europe from Turkey at about the same time, in 1562, and because both shrubs, having hollow and pithy wood, were used by the Turks to make pipes. They were known, respectively, as 'blew pipe' and 'white pipe'. Although knowledgeable botanists separated them into different genera as early as 1623, the white pipe is still frequently referred to as *Syringa*.

The lilacs flower first in late April or May, the common species *Syringa vulgaris* producing dense panicles of richly scented white, yellow, red, blue, or purple single or double flowers. They need a sunny situation but thrive in most soils. There are many varieties, popular among the singles being the wine-red 'Souvenir de Louis Späth', the white 'Vestale', the sky-blue 'Firmament', the rich lilac-red 'Congo', and the soft yellow 'Primrose'. Favourite doubles are the white 'Madame Lemoine', the purple-red 'Charles Joly', the purple-lavender 'Katherine Havemeyer', and the pale pink 'Edward Gardner'.

If later-flowering kinds are favoured, the hybrids of *S. × prestoniae*, commonly called Canadian hybrids, represent a distinct race and flower in June with feathery, graceful, erect or drooping plumes of mostly reddish-purple florets. All lilacs take time to establish so it is advisable to remove flowers appearing in the first season. In later years remove faded flowers as soon as possible after blooming. Always try to purchase plants on their own roots, otherwise you will be for ever plagued by sucker growths from the base. Overgrown bushes can be rejuvenated by cutting the stems back to about 3 ft (1 m) from the ground. They will flower again after two or three years. Propagation can be carried out in late summer from heel cuttings rooted in sand and peat in a propagating frame. Magnesium deficiency sometimes causes lilac leaves to become brittle or blotched with yellow or brown, a condition which can be remedied with dressings of magnesium sulphate (Epsom salts).

Among the mock oranges, *Philadelphus coronarius* makes a dense bushy shrub of 6–9 ft (2–3 m) flowering in June and July. Suitable for full sun or light shade, and thriving in most soils, the exquisite purity of its white cup-shaped flowers and its strong orange-blossom scent make it a summer favourite. Moreover it needs little

The dense, highly fragrant flower panicles of the common lilac (*Syringa vulgaris*)

attention beyond the removal of the old flowering wood when blooming is finished. This species has been grown for centuries and produced some outstanding cultivars. 'Virginal' and 'Enchantment' are both fine semi-doubles; 'Etoile Rose' is white with carmine basal blotches and rich golden stamens; 'Beauclerc' has cerise basal markings; and 'Sybille', which grows only 4 ft (1.2 m) high, bears on arching branches squarish white flowers with purple flushes at the base of the petals. All of these have a rich penetrating scent, discernible at a considerable distance, but upsetting for some people. E. A. Bowles found they gave him hay fever, and either left the country when they were in bloom or had all the buds removed before they opened. The herbalist John Gerard also disliked the scent, which he said 'awakened me from sleepe, so that I could not take any rest till I had cast them out'. There are scentless forms for those so afflicted, also a fine golden-leaved variety called 'Aureus' which keeps its colour best in shade. Propagation is by means of half-ripe cuttings taken in July and August or hardwood cuttings in October and November.

Magnolia grandiflora from the southeastern United States makes a 60–80 ft (18–24 m) tree in its native country, but needs the protection of a warm sunny wall and good but well-drained soil to thrive in northern Europe. It is an impressive evergreen with 6–10 in (15–25 cm) glossy oval leaves, leathery in texture and brown-felted beneath. From June to September, and intermittently into autumn, it carries huge, thick-petalled, bowl-shaped, creamy white flowers. These have a rich spicy fragrance, and are much favoured for floating in flower bowls on dinner tables. However the French botanist André Michaux (1746–1803), who saw trees 70–90 ft (20–27.5 m) high growing in America, said that Indians would not sleep underneath a tree in bloom because the overpowering scent of the flowers could cause death in a single night.

Some aromatic-leaved shrubby plants in character in summer include the Californian laurel (*Umbellularia californica*), an 80 ft (24 m) evergreen which produces yellowish-green flowers in April. The narrow leathery leaves emit when crushed an extremely pungent odour which can cause sneezing and headaches if inhaled too long and deeply.

Laurus nobilis, another evergreen, is the bay laurel of the ancient world. The Romans made it an emblem of victory, and wrapped it around dispatches announcing a victory in battle. During triumphal

A single and a double form of the mock orange (*Philadelphus coronarius*) growing companionably together

marches victorious generals wore laurel crowns on their heads and even the humble soldiers carried a sprig of it in their hands. The bay laurel, which in warm areas will make a small, bushy tree, is native to the Mediterranean region. It also stands clipping well and is frequently fashioned into pyramidal shapes and planted in tubs for formal settings. The aromatic leaves are popular for flavouring stews, soups, and milk puddings.

Other plants with aromatic foliage include rosemary (*Rosmarinus officinalis*), of which there is an upright-growing form as well as the more conventional bush shape; a miscellany of mints, including variegated and golden-leaved forms; thymes, much visited by bees when in flower; and the bog myrtle (*Myrica gale*), a small strongly aromatic deciduous shrub with golden catkins which will grow in acid bogs and swamps where few other plants will survive.

Sweetest of all is the delightful South American lemon verbena (*Lippia citriodora*, syn. *Aloysia triphylla*). Unfortunately, this is not hardy, although I have kept a plant outside, planted against a south wall, for nearly forty years. I cut it fairly hard back in autumn and cover the crown with dry leaves and plastic for winter. Lemon verbena also grows happily in pots and can easily be reproduced from cuttings for that purpose. The mauve flowers are insignificant but the pale green lanceolate leaves impart a most delicious lemon scent to pot-pourri, and can be used for scenting linen or even as a tea substitute.

A plant which is unequivocally associated with summer in most people's minds is the rose. Few gardens are without some representatives of this much-loved, easily grown shrub, which can be used in many situations and will grow in most soils other than the wet and acid. Among several hundred species and thousands of hybrids there are roses suitable for bedding purposes, or for growing in pots and window boxes; climbing varieties to cover walls or train over arches and pergolas; hedging roses; and low suckering types suitable for banks or for edging. All of these flower best in full sun and appreciate regular feeding, particularly an annual mulch of organic material, such as rotted farmyard manure or compost.

Native to the temperate and subtropical regions of the northern hemisphere and of very ancient lineage, roses have always been flowers of luxury. Their scent has been exploited since earliest times. For centuries the fragrance was extracted by steeping the petals in oils and fats, the resulting unguents being used to anoint

RIGHT:
Two beautiful old roses – *Rosa gallica officinalis*, the apothecary's rose, and *R. alba*, the white rose of York

BELOW:
Lemon verbena (*Lippia citriodora*), grown not for its flowers but for its scented foliage

the living and to embalm the dead. Then the technique was discovered of distilling the scent directly from the petals. This find created a great luxury business, particularly in the Middle East, where enormous quantities of scented roses were grown and attar of roses and rose water sent to western Europe. Today the finest attar in the world comes from Bulgaria and a few areas of Turkey, where in a good year 1.5 tonnes of damask-rose petals can be gathered from a single acre. Yet the three million blooms this represents yield only a pint of attar.

If scent is the main reason for growing roses in gardens and there is room for them to develop, no flowers are sweeter than those of the old-fashioned shrub roses, especially those derived from *Rosa gallica*, the musk rose (*R. moschata*), and *R. rugosa*. Many 19th-century hybrids derived from these species display brilliant colours – mauves, magentas, purples, crimsons, and violets – as well as whites and pinks. Their flowers are exquisitely shaped and rounded, the petals springing from a circular central knob. But the stems grow strongly and are also very prickly, so shrub roses are best grown apart from modern varieties. Some of the most fragrant varieties include 'Blanc Double de Coubert', white; 'Cardinal Richelieu', a rich velvety purple; 'Charles de Mills', double, rich crimson and purple; 'Madame Isaac Pereire', double carmine; 'Marie Louise', double, rich pink; 'Roseraie de l'Hay', double, wine-purple; and *Rosa moschata*, single (or sometimes double), white.

Climbing and repeat-flowering roses that have a good scent include 'Compassion', salmon-pink and orange; 'Ena Harkness', crimson scarlet; 'Etoile de Hollande', dark crimson; 'Golden Showers', bright yellow; 'Maigold', yellow with bronze tint; 'New Dawn', blush pink; and 'Zéphirine Drouhin', a thornless variety with deep pink flowers.

Some fine scented floribundas are 'Arthur Bell', bright yellow; 'Harry Edland', deep pink; 'Margaret Merril', blush white; 'Paul Shirville', salmon; and 'Radox Bouquet', warm pink.

Finally, among the scented hybrid teas are 'Alec's Red', rich cherry red; 'Blue Moon', lilac-pink; 'Fragrant Cloud', scarlet; 'Pot o' Gold', old gold; and 'Whisky Mac', amber yellow.

Among summer-blooming border perennials the Chinese paeonies derived from *Paeonia lactiflora* are outstanding for fragrance. Unlike the earlier-blooming European *P. officinalis* forms, which

Fragrant roses

ABOVE LEFT:
'New Dawn', a vigorous, repeat-flowering climber

ABOVE RIGHT:
'Whisky Mac', a hybrid tea – unhappily an unreliable grower

BELOW LEFT:
The ancient rosa mundi (*Rosa gallica versicolor*) reputedly named after Fair Rosamund, mistress of King Henry II

BELOW RIGHT:
'Arthur Bell', a vigorous, exceptionally fragrant, floribunda

have a strong unpleasant smell, the Chinese hybrids possess a rich rose-like scent, and have large, blousy, single or double flowers in a wide range of colours. They grow to a height of $2\frac{1}{2}$–3 ft(75–90 cm), go on for years in the garden, and flower during late May and June. Favourite varieties are 'Bowl of Beauty', a semi-double pink with a central boss of creamy petaloids; 'Cornwall', carmine pink with a cream and rose centre; 'Duchesse de Nemours', a lovely creamy-white; 'Inspecteur Lavergne', double crimson with silver petal tippings; and 'White Wings', single white.

Paeonies need moist but well-drained soil and appreciate sun, provided the buds miss the early morning rays, which can damage them after a frosty night. They are hungry plants, benefitting from annual mulches of rotted compost and dressings of bonemeal, and, for those who want extra plants, can be divided and replanted in September or October. The taller 3–5 ft (90–150 cm) woody-stemmed tree paeonies derived from *P. suffruticosa* are also fragrant,

LEFT:
Irises, phlomis, sweet rockets, lavender, and lady's mantle against the background of the semi-double shrub rose 'Nevada'

BELOW:
A single, pink-flowered paeony, a hybrid garden form of *Paeonia lactiflora*

their huge 5–6 in (13–15 cm) flowers available in pink, salmon, white, or yellow, both singles and doubles. Being grafted plants, with brittle slender stems, they are easily damaged, so should be grown in a protected place in sun or light shade and carefully treated.

Many June-flowering bearded irises are deliciously scented, usually with a rich fruity flavour. There are thousands of named varieties – dwarf, intermediate, and tall – in a wide range of colours or combinations of colours, so if possible make a selection from a nursery when they are in flower. This will disclose their scents as well as their shapes and colours. Bearded irises should be planted in full sun in an open position in well-drained soil, including chalk, prepared with rotted manure or compost and a dressing of bone-meal. Plant them in late June or early July, so that the rhizomatous rootstocks are part showing and with each fan of leaves, shortened by half to prevent wind rocking, facing one way. These irises grow quickly and will need dividing and replanting every second or third year soon after flowering, or the quantity of flowers will lessen. Spring or autumn disturbance can also lose a season's bloom.

The anciently cultivated *I. pallida dalmatica* is another bearded iris worth growing. It is a 3 ft (90 cm) tall plant with silvery leaves, and crinkly, pale mauve and gold-bearded flowers which smell like elderberry blooms. Particularly garden-worthy are its variegated forms, 'Argenteo-variegata' with silver-striped foliage and 'Aureo-variegata' with golden stripes.

Another old and much-loved plant is the 2 ft (60 cm) white-blossomed *I. florentina* – a form of *I. germanica* – whose dried rhizomes are the source of the violet-scented orris powder, although, according to Alice Coats, 'the fragrance does not appear until the roots are quite dry, and is not fully developed until they are two years old'. Orris is used for scenting toilet items, sachets, pot-pourri, and tooth powders. It is also the basis of certain cheap perfumes and is cultivated for that purpose in southern Europe.

We also have a native iris in *I. foetidissima*, more familiarly known as stinking gladdon or roast-beef plant, on account of the aroma released by its bruised leaves, which you may or may not find agreeable. It is a plant for the shadiest, most out-of-the-way place in the garden. The main reason for growing it is neither the smell, nor its mauve and yellow flowers, but its decorative seed pods, bursting with scarlet seeds in autumn.

'Shepherd's Delight' – an exquisite hybrid bearded iris with a fruity scent

LEFT:
The hardy tree paeony 'L'Esperance' – a *Paeonia lutea* hybrid with very large, semi-double flowers

BELOW:
Paeonia lactiflora 'Bowl of Beauty' – a large, early, herbaceous paeony with scented blooms

Another perennial which has a pleasing scent is *Aruncus dioicus* (*A. sylvester*), the false goat's beard, which has a clean smell reminiscent of new-mown hay. Suitable for most soils, it grows 6–7 ft (1.8–2.1 m) high, with broad ferny leaves and large creamy–yellow plumes of feathery flowers. It makes a fine specimen plant to grow by itself on a lawn, but also associates pleasantly in mixed borders with plants such as delphiniums, blue campanulas, and astilbes. Male and female flowers are borne on separate plants, the former producing the finest and largest plumes.

Daylilies (*Hemerocallis* species) may have earned their name because of the short existence of their individual blooms, but modern hybrids provide such a succession that the lily–like flowers appear sporadically over a long period. Many have a faint scent, particularly the European *H. flava*, which has a fragrance like honeysuckle. Easy to grow in moist soil and sun or partial shade, modern hybrid daylilies have arching grassy leaves. Today it

RIGHT:
A striped form of burning bush, *Dictamnus albus* 'Purpurea'

BELOW:
A cluster of scented daylilies (*Hemerocallis flava*)

PAGES 92–3
LEFT:
The lacy beauty of a 'Old Crimson Clove', a 16th-century pink or gillyflower

RIGHT:
The bunched flowerheads of another very old cottage-garden plant, the sweet william (*Dianthus barbatus*)

is possible to obtain varieties with yellow and orange blooms, also various shades between pink and red as well as bicolours. The Chinese have long eaten the dried buds and flowers as a vegetable.

Dictamnus albus, the burning bush or fraxinella, is a plant that resents being constantly disturbed, yet lives many years if happily situated. Growing 2–3 ft (60–90 cm) tall, with spikes of white or mauve-purple, long-stamened flowers and ash-leaved foliage, the plants are aromatic in all their parts due to the presence of a volatile oil. If a lighted taper is brought close to a seed head it will ignite without harming the plant. This does not work in damp weather – the seed head has to be quite dry. Graham Thomas, an authority on roses and one of Britain's leading flower artists, suggests bringing the spikes indoors first to dry, then they will explode in the flame and shoot out the seeds.

Pinks and border carnations, especially the old, 16th-century clove carnations, are powerfully fragrant. The clove carnation, with its dark red flowers, is derived from *Dianthus caryophyllus*; it was at one time used for flavouring ales and wines, hence its English name 'sops-in-wine'. The smaller pinks, derived from *D. plumarius*, received their name from their jagged petal edges, which reminded early botanists of the cuts made by pinking scissors on Tudor garments.

Today there are many races and varieties of pinks and carnations, variously coloured and generally fragrant. *D. barbatus*, the sweet william, is another scented species, with its flowers growing in bunched heads. It is a popular biennial, raised from seed.

Other scented perennials for summer borders include monardas, especially the variety *Monarda didyma* 'Cambridge Scarlet', which grows 2–3 ft (60–90 cm) high and whose square stems carry whorls of scarlet, nettle-shaped flowers and aromatic nettle-shaped leaves. It grows happily in either sun or shade provided, that its feet are in soil that is always moist.

Phlox paniculata hybrids appear late in the summer, but are certainly the showiest members of the large phlox family, with their 3–4 ft (90–120 cm) stems carrying heavy, sweetly scented trusses of red, white, mauve, or purple flowers, usually with eyes of a contrasting colour. However, these phlox are among the earliest plants in the garden to show signs of drought, so they may need watering in dry weather.

RIGHT:
The lavender-like flower spikes of catmint (*Nepeta × faasenii*)

BELOW:
Phlox paniculata hybrids bearing their large, fragrant flower trusses

The catmint *Nepeta* × *faassenii* does indeed attract cats, which like to roll in the plants and chew the aromatic foliage. Under favourable circumstances the plant, with its pale mauve flowers, makes an attractive edging for sunny, well-drained situations.

Several woody-stemmed perennials are also effective in mixed borders, especially *Lavandula spica*, a plant which has pleasantly fragrant leaves and flowers. *Santolina chamaecyparissus*, the lavender cotton, is a lime-loving perennial for hot, dry soils, with silvery, finely cut aromatic leaves and, in late summer, masses of golden, button-shaped flower heads. Another species, *S. neapolitana* (*S. rosmarinifolia*), with pale yellow flowers, has grey leaves which smell most unpleasant.

Much sweeter are the aromatic leaves of a ground-hugging cranesbill from southern Europe, *Geranium macrorrhizum*. Semi-evergreen and suitable for most soils in sun or shade, it makes an attractive, weed-smothering ground cover. The rounded but divided leaves scent the hand that touches them.

A decorative variety, *Salvia officinalis* 'Tricolor', of the commonly grown culinary sage

Salvia officinalis, the culinary sage, and its variously coloured foliage varieties, have aromatic foliage. So, too, do several other sages. The large, triangular leaves of the clary, *S. sclarea*, a hardy biennial, yield by distillation a muscat scent that is used commercially in perfumes and to flavour some German wines. The clary produces striking $2\frac{1}{2}$ ft (75 cm) flower spikes composed of purple or yellow bracts. The Vatican sage (*S. turkestanica*) is so powerfully aromatic that even to brush against the plant transfers its scent, which then persists for several hours. *S. nemorosa*, a popular blue-flowered border perennial, and *S. rutilans*, with red flowers, are also aromatic; the leaves of the latter when crushed being reminiscent of pineapple.

Calamintha nepetoides, a small perennial with soft lilac, lavender-like blooms, has a long flowering season, and a minty smell when the leaves are crushed. It is frequently planted between paving stones to exploit this characteristic, a trick also practised with dwarf thyme (*Thymus serpyllum*), chamomile (*Anthemis nobilis*), and the

BELOW LEFT:
Salvia officinalis 'Icterine', a variegated culinary sage

BELOW RIGHT:
Clary sage (*Salvia clarea*), the source of an aromatic oil used in perfumery

Corsican mint (*Mentha requienii*), a tiny mauve-flowered perennial which releases a strong peppermint smell when trodden on.

A number of annuals can be included in summer displays, particularly for borders, window boxes, and even hanging baskets. The half-hardy kinds need to be started under glass and planted outside when weather conditions allow, whereas the hardy annuals can be sown where they are to flower, either in spring or late summer. The common name often reveals whether a plant is scented. Some obvious examples are sweet pea (*Lathyrus odoratus* hybrids), sweet sultan (*Centaurea moschata*), sweet rocket (*Hesperis matronalis*), sweet alyssum (*Lobularia* (*Alyssum*) *maritimum*), sweet-scented catchfly (*Silene armeria*), and sweet-scented marigold (*Tagetes lucida*), all of which are grown as hardy annuals.

However there are other scented hardy or half-hardy, biennial, or even perennial, plants that can easily be raised from seed. Examples are *Lupinus luteus*, a rich yellow, half-hardy, fragrant lupin of

RIGHT:
'Painted Lady', a Victorian variety of the ever-popular sweet pea (*Lathyrus odoratus*)

BELOW:
The stock-like flowers of sweet rocket or dame's violet (*Hesperis matronalis*), which are highly fragrant in the evening

The sweet-scented, sticky-leaved catchfly
(*Silene armeria*)

PAGES 102–103
LEFT:
Goat's rue (*Galega officinalis*) – a sturdy
plant for the back of a mixed border

RIGHT:
A gaily-coloured group of pot marigolds
(*Calendula officinalis*)

1–2 ft (30–60 cm); *Heliotropium arborescens*, the old-fashioned cherry pie, with royal purple, richly scented flowers; *Gilia tricolor*, a hardy annual with blue, golden, and purple flowers which smell of chocolate; *Galega officinalis*, goat's rue, a perennial with lavender-blue or white flowers; and antirrhinums, commonly called snapdragons, which have a strong, sweet smell and are obtainable in various colours, shapes, and heights, and are usually treated as hardy or half-hardy annuals. Then there are the pot marigold (*Calendula officinalis*), popular as a cut flower, and the mignonette (*Reseda odorata*) both of which are strongly scented and grown as hardy annuals; the violet cress (*Ionopsidium acaule*); a vast number of nasturtiums (*Tropaeolum majus* cultivars); and the poached-egg flower (*Limnanthes douglasii*).

Stocks, too, are raised from seed – *Matthiola bicornis*, the small night-flowering, clove-scented kind, as well as the taller and more elegant Brompton and East Lothian stocks derived from *M. incana*.

RIGHT:
Night-flowering stocks (*Matthiola bicornis*), here mingled with pinks and double stocks

BELOW:
Mignonette (*Reseda odorata*), whose scent was described by its first English grower, Philip Miller, as 'very like fresh raspberries'

Petunias, such as *Petunia multiflorus* and *P.* × *hybrida*, have to be treated as half-hardy, as does *Nicotiana alata*, the flowering, often night-scented, tobacco plant, although *Oenothera missouriensis*, an evening primrose, is a hardy perennial.

There are also some splendid bulbous plants for summer enjoyment, particularly among the lilies. One of the easiest and most reliable is *Lilium regale*, a lovely, richly scented species, discovered by E. H. Wilson on the borderland of China and Tibet in 1904. It was growing there in tens of thousands and must have presented a remarkable sight. It has never been discovered anywhere else. Today there are variously coloured forms of this lily; they are all stem rooters and so should be planted 6–9 in (15–23 cm) deep to allow for this, and they should be grown in well-drained soil in sun or light shade. Propagation by division should be carried out soon after flowering, but they also do well from seeds, frequently flowering in two years from sowing or occasionally in one year.

LEFT:
The flowers of *Limnanthes douglasii* that give the plant its popular name of poached-egg plant

BELOW:
Tropaeolum majus 'Alaska', a good variegated variety of nasturtium

Another well-known species is the European *L. candidum*, the white-flowered madonna lily, cultivated since the days of the Cretan civilizations (*c.* 1750 BC), and in Britain probably since Roman times. Growing 3–6 ft (90–180 cm) high, they carry many wide-open, heavily scented, glistening white flowers with golden stamens on each leafy stem. The species grows well in limy soils, but needs sun. It must be planted out in late July or August, at a period when its bulbs are dormant – soon after blooming is finished and before the overwintering basal leaves appear in September. The bulbs should be planted shallowly, so that their tops are only just below soil level. A temperamental species, it thrives in some gardens but fails in others, so successful colonies are best left alone.

Many other lilies grow well between herbaceous perennials. Among the most reliable of the scented kinds are the lime-loving *L. henryi*, an August bloomer with 8 ft (2.4 m) arching stems of nodding, apricot-yellow Turk's cap flowers; *L. speciosum*, white

RIGHT:
Oenothera missouriensis, one of the evening primroses that make fragrant the dusks of summer

BELOW:
The tobacco plant (*Nicotiana affinis*), which gives off its sweetest scent in the evening

with pink or crimson markings on 6 ft (1.8 m) stems in late summer; and *L. auratum*, perhaps the finest of all the lilies, with very large, 8 in (20 cm) thick-petalled, funnel-shaped flowers, white with yellow or crimson markings on 6–8 ft (1.8–2.4 m) stems. All these are stem rooters, so need deep planting with moist, rich growing conditions, good drainage, and full sun.

Alstroemerias, although commonly called Peruvian lilies, belong to the daffodil family. The easiest to grow is the orange-flowered *Alstroemeria aurantiaca*, a native of Chile, with bunched heads of small, lily-shaped, flaming orange flowers on every wiry 3 ft (90 cm) stem. In a sunny, sheltered position and in well-drained soil this species can become a nuisance; it spreads by means of underground stolons to positions where it is not wanted. The fragrant, pink-bloomed *A. ligtu*, 3–4 ft (90–120 cm), was introduced from the Andes in the 1920s and later crossed with the red *A. haemantha*, also from the Andes, to produce the Ligtu hybrids, a race with a delightful blend of colour forms in shades of cream, pink, rose, salmon, and orange with dark markings. All of these are pleasantly scented, ideal for cutting, and make handsome border perennials. They bloom in early summer, spread slowly by means of seed or running roots, and have the curious distinction of carrying their leaves upside down, on account of the leaf stalks having a twist in them which brings the undersides uppermost. Plant the dormant roots about 6 in (15 cm) deep and gradually earth them up as they grow.

The summer hyacinth, *Galtonia (Hyacinthus) candicans*, is also fragrant; its 3–4 ft (90–120 cm) stems carry spikes of white, dark-stamened flowers at a time when border plants are scarce. They look well between bearded irises, having complementary glaucous strap-like leaves, or alongside shrubs in any sunny, well-drained situation. A few gladioli are fragrant, particularly members of the sun-loving, cream-flowered species *Gladiolus tristis* and its South African-raised varieties.

Hostas (also known as funkias or plantain lilies) are handsome, compact, and imposing plants for key positions in shady places or to grow as container specimens. The broad, handsome foliage comes in a variety of shapes and shades, very many being variegated, and accompanies lily-shaped, white, lilac, or deep purple flowers. A few are sweetly fragrant, particularly *Hosta plantaginea*, which is white and lily-scented, and a taller variety, 'Royal Standard'.

The shrubby, late-blooming yuccas (palm lilies) are American

RIGHT:
The freckled, fragrant blossom of the golden-rayed lily (*Lilium auratum*)

PAGES 112–13
LEFT:
The Peruvian lily (*Alstroemeria aurantiaca*) – not a member of the lily family, but so called because of its lily-like flowers

RIGHT:
The scented white flower bells of the summer hyacinth (*Galtonia candicans*)

evergreens with stout, sword-like leaves growing 4–6 ft (1.2–1.8 m) tall and arranged in dense clumps, often on woody trunks. In late summer they produce giant plumes of white, cream, or greenish flowers. Afterwards the flower spikes die, to be replaced by a fresh shoot which may take several years to produce further blooms. Well-drained soil and full sun are essential, and new plants can either be raised from imported seeds or reproduced from side shoots below the soil of an existing plant, detached and grown on in a greenhouse. The most fragrant species include the 4–5 ft (1.2–1.5 m) cream-flowered *Yucca filamentosa*, which is deliciously fragrant in the evenings.

Fragrant climbing plants are particularly appreciated on summer evenings, for they raise the blooms to different levels. Honeysuckles, or woodbines as they are often called, are especially welcome, but not all of them are fragrant, so it is advisable to check on this point before purchase. Some scented honeysuckles that

The beautiful, and reliably fragrant, honeysuckle *Lonicera × americana*

never fail to please, though, are *Lonicera × americana*, a beautiful climber with whorls of yellow flowers; *L. caprifolium*, deciduous, with whorls of near-white flowers tinged with pink; *L. hildebrandiana*, very vigorous in sheltered spots, with paired white blooms that become orange with age; and *L. japonica*, heavily scented, white-flowered evergreen, and very robust, which grows, in time, to 20–30 ft (6–9 m) (ignore the golden-mottled form, which does not flower sufficiently freely for a climbing honeysuckle). *L. periclymenum*, our native woodbine, with its whorls of yellowish-white flowers splashed with red that give off a scent that is particularly strong in the evenings, is another good choice. There are several forms, of which 'Belgica', the Dutch honeysuckle, has a bushier habit. The hybrid *L. × tellmanniana* is a beautiful deciduous hybrid with heads of rich yellow, red-tipped flowers. All honeysuckles appreciate light shade and moist, rich soil.

Jasmines are frequently fragrant and easily cultivated in good

BELOW:
A cloud of white, perfumed blossom – *Clematis recta*, growing here alongside *Alchemilla mollis*

PAGES 116–17
LEFT:
The cowslip-scented *Clematis rehderiana*, which flowers in autumn

RIGHT:
A fragrant cluster of wisteria blossom

garden soil and sun. They need scant attention beyond periodic thinning and can be propagated from cuttings. The white-flowered deciduous *Jasminum officinale* is one of the easiest; grown near the house, it is particularly pleasant on summer evenings. It has a golden leaf-blotched form 'Aureum', which I find equally hardy and adaptable. *J. × stephanense*, with terminal clusters of pink flowers, is also fragrant, but needs more shelter than *J. officinale*.

Most large-flowered clematis are scentless; it is the small-bloomed species that are, frequently, fragrant. *Clematis montana* hybrids are robust and free flowering and several have a delightful scent. The white-flowered 'Alexander' and the pink 'Elizabeth' are both fragrant, but the most outstanding scent-wise is 'Wilsonii', a cream variety with twisted sepals, rather later than the others, and so strongly scented that it can be detected 15–20 yd (14–18 m) away. Others to note are *C. flammula*, the virgin's bower, which bears small white almond-scented blooms in late summer and the

RIGHT:
The sword-like aromatic leaves of the variegated sweet flag (*Acorus calamus* 'Variegatus')

BELOW:
Escallonia macrantha, a good shrub for the seaside, with glossy green leaves

Akebia quinata, a hardy, semi-evergreen, tall-growing climber

cowslip-scented *C. rehderiana*. Try, too, the hardy, lime-tolerant herbaceous border plants *C. davidiana* (*C. heracleifolia*), which grows 3–4 ft (90–12 cm) tall and is blue flowered; *C. recta*, 3 ft (90 cm), white; and *C. viticella*, a cream-coloured climber of 10–20 ft (3–6 m).

There are very many climbing roses, some of which can be grown with *Clematis jackmanii* hybrids, the former supporting the latter and both of them flowering at different seasons. Early in the year these clematis can be cut hard back to 12 in (30 cm) or 18 in (45 cm) from the ground. New shoots will grow up while the roses are in bloom, and when these start to fade the clematis come into their own.

A few other fragrant climbers may be noted here. Both the lilac and the white forms of *Wisteria sinensis* are almost overpowering at times. *Akebia quinata*, a slender twiner which will grow in deep shade, has pendent sprays of fragrant purple flowers, which, if both male and female plants are grown, develop purplish sausage-shaped fruits in autumn. *Escallonia macrantha* has small, rose-crimson flowers and glossy aromatic leaves.

Even water gardens have scented plants, particularly the hardy water lilies derived from the fragrant North American species *Nymphaea odorata*, like the lovely 'Pink Opal', and most tropical tender species and varieties, like the night-blooming 'Red Flare'. Aquatics include *Mimulus ringens*, mauve-flowered with sweetly aromatic foliage; *Acorus calamus*, with aromatic-when-bruised leaves and rootstocks; the water hawthorn (*Aponogeton distachyus*), with scented white flowers; and *Cotula coronopifolia*, with its lemon-scented leaves.

AUTUMN RIPENESS

Chrysanthemum parthenium, feverfew

AUTUMN DOES NOT PROVIDE the sweet elusive scents of spring, for it is a season of maturity, where, in field and garden alike, one can sense the year's fulfillment by the rich aromas of ripening fruits. Nonetheless, autumn-flowering trees, perennials, and bulbs are still providing colour and scent.

A few bulbous plants are outstanding at this time of year. The most striking of these is *Acidanthera bicolor* 'Murielae', which belongs to the gladiolus family, and indeed is sometimes known as *Gladiolus callianthus*. Although known since 1896, this large-flowered clone was rediscovered in the Highlands of Ethiopia in the 1930s by the then British Consul, who named it after his wife. It is a graceful, grassy-leaved plant of 2½–3 ft (75–90 cm). Each flowering stem bears eight to ten starry, snow-white flowers with crimson basal blotches, about 3 in (7.5 cm) across and richly scented. The plant is hardy only in sunny sheltered gardens, where it makes a perfect associate for the rosy pink *Nerine bowdenii*. Plant the corms 5 in (12.5 cm) deep in spring, protecting them with a cloche if necessary, or start them in pots in warmth (60° F, 16° C) and plant them out when weather conditions are favourable. In cooler areas they should be lifted and stored like gladioli, when they have finished blooming.

Crinums are South African plants with very large bulbs and long, floppy, strap-shaped leaves. The only one hardy enough for British gardens is *C. × powellii*, a hybrid with stout, 4 ft (1.2 m) stems terminating in umbels of funnel-shaped pink or white flowers, which open in succession so that the decorative period is prolonged. The white form is much the most attractive and makes a long-lasting cut flower. Plant the bulbs in a warm sunny corner with only their tips protruding. My own plants, which have been established more than thirty years, are lightly protected with leaves or a lean-to frame in winter, mainly because some of the bulb tips protrude up to 22 in (56 cm) above the ground. Propagate by division.

An autumn bulb with an interesting history is *Crocus sativus*, the celebrated saffron crocus, which flowers in September and October. The small, fragrant, violet-purple flowers with their rich golden stamens are only a few inches high, but *en masse* they can be quite spectacular.

A small hardy cyclamen with fragrant flowers is the autumn-

ABOVE RIGHT:
Cyclamen hederaefolium – 'this little frightened cyclamen'

BELOW RIGHT:
Crinum × powellii, whose drooping, trumpet-shaped blooms make long-lasting cut flowers

The superbly graceful, richly scented
gladiolus *Acidanthera bicolor* 'Murielae'

blooming *Cyclamen hederaefolium* (*C. neapolitanum*). An easy little free-flowering plant, it carries pink or white blooms with turned-up petals and was graphically described by Vita Sackville West as 'this little frightened cyclamen, with leveret ears laid back'. The flowers appear before the leaves from round, solid tubers which can grow as large as a hat in time. Later, green and white variegated leaves appear – no two exactly alike – while the stems of fading flowers curl up like watch springs, dragging the pods with their maturing seeds down into the soil. And so the plants spread, making a handsome ground cover in sun or shade, but especially attractive underneath large deciduous trees.

Among herbaceous perennials there are various autumn-flowering composites with scented flowers or leaves – sometimes both. Most do well in any good garden soil and can be increased by division or seed.

They include a number of florist's chrysanthemums and *Chrysanthemum balsamita*, the costmary or alecost, so called because the leaves were once used to impart a balsamic flavour to ale. John Parkinson described this as one of the sweetest of herbs, recommending that it be 'tied up with lavender to lie upon beds or pillows'. It grows to 2–3 ft (60–90 cm) and has small, neat leaves and numerous yellow tansy-like flowers. *C. parthenium*, the feverfew, has very strongly scented flowers and leaves. It grows to the same height and has much-branched stems with small white daisy flowers. The double form 'White Bonnet' and the single, gold-leaved 'Aureum' are popular bedding plants.

Achilleas have larger and showier flowers, especially *Achillea eupatorium* (*A. filipendula*), which has large, flat, plate-like heads composed of myriads of small golden flowers. These are frequently dried for winter bouquets and the pungent leaves used in potpourris. It grows to 3–4 ft (90–120 cm).

Monardas are among the most colourful late bloomers for moist, sunny borders. *Monarda didyma* 'Cambridge Scarlet' is particularly bright, and white, pink, and purple forms are also available. All grow to about 3 ft (90 cm) and have sage-like flowers arranged in a succession of whirls around the square stems. The species is sometimes called Oswego tea, because the sweet-smelling leaves were used as a substitute for tea in the American town of that name.

Then there are hosts of culinary herbs such as mints (*Mentha* species), some of which have variegated or golden leaves, and

RIGHT:
The daisy-like flowers of feverfew (*Chrysanthemum parthenium*) rising above its aromatic leaves

BELOW:
Alecost or costmary (*Chrysanthemum balsamita*), once used for flavouring beer

savory (*Satureja montana*), which retains its aromatic fragrance all winter. This is sometimes boiled with broad beans in the same way that mint is added to peas and new potatoes.

Ancient Greek physicians held high opinions of the virtues of sage (*Salvia officinalis*), a plant frequently still flowering in autumn. Apart from the grey-green foliage of the species there are forms with variously coloured leaves – reddish-purple, green and gold, green and white, and a tricoloured variety patterned with cream, red, and grey-green. There are also varieties with white or yellow flowers instead of purple.

Other herbs with fragrant foliage include hyssop (*Hyssopus officinalis*), a 2 ft (60 cm) evergreen with sweetly scented pink, white, or blue flowers. Both leaves and flowers can be used in pot-pourri. *Teucrium chamaedrys* is the germander, an old evergreen strewing herb popular in Tudor times, with pink flowers, 6–8 in (15–20 cm) tall. *Nepeta × faassenii* (often mistakenly called

LEFT:
Monarda didyma 'Cambridge Scarlet', the sweet bergamot or bee balm

BELOW:
The flat, plate-like flowerheads of *Achillea filipendulina*

N. mussinii) has pungent leaves that are irresistible to cats and 12 in (30 cm) spikes of lavender-blue flowers in summer. This plant needs a warm situation and well-drained soil. All these herbs are propagated by seeds or cuttings.

One of the most useful shrubs for 'peace' pillows and pot-pourri is the Chilean lemon verbena, *Lippia citriodora*, now ready for harvesting. It is deciduous, with privet-like leaves arranged in threes at intervals along the stems. These are deliciously fragrant with a strong lemon scent, for which reason they are sometimes used to make a refreshing drink, but the small, pale purple flowers, in panicles at the tops of the stems, are insignificant. A warm sunny corner and well-drained soil is essential for plants grown outdoors, plus winter protection in very severe weather, or they can be grown in a greenhouse. They attain a height of 6–15 ft (2–4.5 m), according to situation.

Osmanthus heterophyllus (*O. ilicifolius*) is an attractive evergreen shrub with a dense bushy habit, ultimately reaching 10 ft (3 m) in height. It is frequently mistaken for holly, so similarly shaped are its leaves, especially as some species are spiny edged. Its small, white, fragrant flowers grow in 1 in (2.5 cm) clusters, appearing in September and October. In its native Japan they are succeeded by blue oblong fruits, but these rarely occur in Britain. It will grow in sun or partial shade in any well-drained soil protected from north and east winds. The plant is sometimes used for hedging purposes. Propagation is by half-ripe cuttings rooted in a propagating frame in July or by layers pegged down in September.

Elaeagnus pungens, also Japanese, is a robust, spreading evergreen with thorny stems. It will grow to 10 ft (3 m) in time unless controlled by cutting. It bears many glossy, leathery, green leaves with white undersides. Fragrant, silvery white, tubular flowers appear in clusters in October and November. The variety 'Maculata', with conspicuous golden splashes on the leaves, is slower growing but very striking at all seasons, particularly in winter. It also cuts well for indoor decoration. It is propagated by cuttings taken in late August and rooted in a cold frame.

The Spanish broom (*Spartium junceum*) is a hardy deciduous shrub. It has few leaves – the green rush-like stems take on most of the leaf functions. It is a straggly shrub of 8–12 ft (2.5–3.5 m), colourful when in flower between June and September. Blooms are pea-shaped, 1 in (2.5 cm) long, rich yellow, and sweetly scented.

ABOVE LEFT:
The winter savory (*Satureja montana*), which retains its fragrance all through the winter months

BELOW LEFT:
The wall germander (*Teucrium chamaedrys*) – a favourite herb for a knot garden

This is an admirable plant for hot dry banks, although it is best if a lower-growing shrub can be planted in front to mask its bare base. Propagate from seeds raised in pots, because these plants resent too much root disturbance. In southern Europe the flowers are used in perfumery.

Perovskia atriplicifolia from Afghanistan is a small shrubby perennial with ovate leaves smelling of sage. Growing 3–5 ft (90–150 cm) tall, it is deciduous, producing in August and September terminal panicles of tubular, two-lipped, violet-blue flowers. Grow it in sun and any well-drained soil, including chalk. The old dead stems should be retained in winter as protection, then cut back to ground level in spring. It is propagated from heel cuttings in July in a cold frame.

Artemisia abrotanum is the southernwood, also known to country folk as lad's love and old man. Its silvery-grey, finely cut foliage is richly aromatic. It has been cultivated in Britain ever since the 16th

RIGHT:
Perovskia atriplicifolia – aromatic grey leaves and small blue flowers

BELOW:
The gold-splashed leaves of *Elaeagnus pungens* 'Maculata', which bears fragrant tubular flowers in late autumn

century. On account of its strong scent it was commonly used in nosegays and as a moth repellent, which probably accounts for the old French name of 'Garde-robe'. The herbalist Nicholas Culpeper (1616–54) recommended ashes of southernwood mixed with oil as a cure for baldness. The yellow, button-like flowers appear in September to October. Plants should be grown in sun and well-drained soil, and may be propagated by heel cuttings.

Another artemisia sometimes obtainable from nurseries is *A. tridentata*, the sage brush of the western United States of America. Evergreen, it has wedge-shaped leaves of varying sizes which release a strong, pleasant scent, most marked after rain and strong enough to scent the air for several yards around.

Jasminum officinale is the common white jasmine, cultivated since time immemorial for its deliciously fragrant white blossoms. Although sometimes grown as a bush, pruned back each spring, it makes a fine wall shrub, growing up to 30 ft (9 m) in favoured situ-

LEFT:
The beautiful white, scented flowers of *Jasminum officinale*

BELOW:
Southernwood (*Artemisia abrotanum*), here growing at the front of a border

ations. The pinnate leaves are deciduous, with five, seven, or nine leaflets; the flowers are in 2–3 in (5–7 cm) axillary clusters from June to October. A variety with heavy yellow blotches on the leaves called 'Aureum' is as hardy as the type; both are propagated from nodal cuttings in late summer.

The passion flower belongs to a very extensive family but only *Passiflora caerulea* is hardy. To succeed it needs a sheltered, well-drained position in sun or partial shade, and to be grown on a trellis which has a wall backing. Even then it needs a warm, sheltered spot, although it makes a good climber for a cool greenhouse or glass extension. This species has palmate leaves, and delicately scented 4 in (10 cm) flowers with white petals, golden stamens, and blue-purple filaments, followed in a good season by golden-yellow, egg-shaped fruits. It can be increased from seed or by cuttings rooted in a propagating frame with bottom heat. Although passion-flower blooms are short lived – usually dying the second day – they appear in quick succession from June until October.

WINTERSWEET

Daphne mezereum, mezereon

WINTER IN THE GARDEN is not the dead season it often seems. If one grows winter-flowering plants there is still plenty to see and enjoy. Curiously, too, a surprising number of winter blooms are scented. One wonders why this should be when few flying insects are in evidence in cold weather. What is the purpose of flower fragrance other than to attract insect pollinators?

How, for that matter, is scent produced by plants? Organic chemists say fragrance is due to the presence of various chemical compounds and a complex manufacturing process. But what is the explanation of the mystery of the scented musk, which has puzzled people for years? This North American creeping plant, *Mimulus moschatus*, with sweetly scented yellow flowers and sticky hairy leaves, was widely grown as a pot plant is the last century. Its scent was apparently rich and penetrating, capable of filling a room with fragrance. Then, just before World War I, this characteristic disappeared – everywhere and quite suddenly. According to William Robinson, in *The English Flower Garden*, there were originally two strains of this musk, one fragrant and the other scentless. Some constitutional weakness caused the former to die out, while the scentless race still thrives.

To make the most of the necessarily limited number of scented shrubs and plants available for a winter garden, it is advisable to spread them thinly or else grow them in groups between other plants. This will not only frame them with a pleasant background but make the most of their scents. Plants likely to be in flower between late November and February, but not necessarily fragrant, include certain varieties of *Erica carnea* heathers, camellias, hellebores, and winter pansies, and there will, of course, be a number of evergreens.

Among the scented flowering shrubs viburnums are undoubtedly the longest in bloom and the most useful. Best of them all is the Chinese *Viburnum farreri* (*V. fragrans*). It was introduced in 1914 by the plant hunter Reginald Farrer (1880–1920), who found plants growing in Chinese cottage gardens at an altitude so exposed that corn apparently only ripens there one year in three. Not surprisingly, therefore, *V. farreri* is quite frost-resistant. In my own garden a hedge of it was planted more than sixty years ago by previous tenants. This hedge is now some 12 ft (3 m) high, and, apart from a

Viburnum farreri, one of the longest-flowering of scented shrubs

light clipping each autumn, receives no attention and has never given us any trouble. The species makes an upright, rather dense shrub with small neat leaves and from late October until the end of March produces bursts of small, sweetly scented flowers in terminal and lateral clusters on the naked branches. These flowers are white in bud but open pink and are so richly fragrant that on a fine day their presence can be detected at a distance of several yards. Propagation is easily effected by rooting half-ripe cuttings in sandy soil around July.

V. × bodnantense is a hybrid of *V. farreri* with *V. grandiflorum*, another Chinese species with larger and longer flower clusters.

Another Chinese shrub, *Chimonanthus praecox* (*C. fragrans*), is the wintersweet, a slow grower – reaching 4 × 3 ft (1.2 m × 90 cm) after five years – but worth all the care in the world because the fragrance of its flowers is so rich and powerful that a small spray will scent a large room. Michael Haworth-Booth, the veteran shrub

Wintersweet (*Chimonanthus praecox*), which bears its waxy flowers on its bare stems

expert, said of it 'No nose that has ever smelt it in unsullied youth, can ever forget it, even in extreme old age'. The blooms, which appear on the naked branches in late winter, are bell-shaped and pendent, of a waxy lemon-yellow colour relieved by purple anthers. This is the only species, but *C. praecox* has a variety, 'Grandiflorus', with larger, deeper yellow, red-stained flowers and another, 'Luteus', of a clear, waxy yellow.

Although wintersweet will grow on chalk it is not hardy in cold wet soils or exposed situations, and if possible should be planted against a warm wall or fence in well-drained soil. Propagation is by means of half-ripe cuttings taken in mid-summer. In China the flower sprays are used by ladies to adorn their hair, while the twigs and prunings, which are also aromatic, are made into bundles to scent clothes, closets, and cupboards.

Hamamelis virginiana, the American witch hazel, has only a faint sweet scent and its flowers make little show. Yet it is important as the source of commercial witch hazel, an extract from the bark having been used for centuries by Amerindians for healing wounds. A far better plant for the garden is the Chinese witch hazel, *H. mollis*, which E. A. Bowles called the Epiphany plant, partly because its flowering time coincides with that Christian festival, but also because it provides the gifts of the Magi – gold in the colour of its flowers, frankincense in its sweet scent, and myrrh from the presence of a bitter principle in the bark.

H. mollis makes a large and spreading deciduous shrub with soft hairy leaves and large, golden-yellow, raggle-taggle, spidery flowers, which are highly fragrant and cling to the bare branches from December to March. Another desirable character is the golden-orange hue assumed in autumn by the foliage prior to leaf fall. There are several varieties, of which the finest is 'Pallida', which has large pompon-like blooms composed of myriads of sulphur-yellow, strap-shaped petals. 'Brevipetala' has orange-bronze flowers and 'Jelena', a copper-red variety derived from *H. × intermedia* (which has *H. mollis* as one parent), is colourful and unusual but less fragrant. All the witch hazels should be planted in good soil in full sun or light shade. An annual mulch with rotted compost is recommended to keep the soil moist and friable and to feed the plant roots.

Although *Abeliophyllum distichum* came from its native Korea in 1924, it is still scarcely known or grown. This is probably because it

RIGHT:
The exquisitely scented Chinese witch hazel, *Hamamelis mollis*

BELOW:
Abeliophyllum distichum – a close relative of forsythia

does not thrive as a free-standing shrub. Accordingly it is advisable to plant it against a warm wall, possibly a house wall, in order to appreciate its almond scent and winter flowers. It is not a rampant climber, 6–8 ft (1.8–2.4 m) being its normal height, but it is suitable for most soils except the alkaline. Closely related to forsythia (and sometimes called the white forsythia), it bears its white, pink-tinged flowers in bunches on the bare branches in late winter. The leaves are ovate and opposite, on both surfaces. Frequent stem removal by fairly severe pruning soon after flowering is advisable.

Azaras are evergreen shrubs from Chile and Argentina and accordingly likely to be tender in all but favoured localities. Yet, given the right conditions and some form of winter protection, they are very rewarding, with their small, glossy, usually oval leaves and grouped clusters of vanilla-scented, yellow flowers between January and March. These are borne in great profusion and so provide plenty of colour, although they are petal-less – it is the long stamens that provide the display.

The Christmas box, *Sarcococca confusa*, bearing its modest, petal-less flowers

A. dentata grows 8–12 ft (2.4–3.6 m) high and needs well-drained soil and a sheltered position in full sun or light shade. The minimum winter temperature it will stand is 23° F (−5° C). Container-grown specimens are reputed to have a better chance of establishing than plants from the open ground. The hardiest species is *A. microphylla*. The flowers appear in February and are so richly scented that their presence can be detected yards away from the shrub or tree. 'Variegata' is similar but with cream variegations on the leaves.

Azaras need little or no pruning beyond cutting out any winter-damaged wood and can be propagated from softwood cuttings taken in spring or mid-summer.

Sarcococcas are too often overlooked, yet they are useful shade shrubs for small gardens, and being native to the Himalayas and China are quite hardy. They are neat, narrow-leaved evergreens belonging to the box family – their common names are sweet box or Christmas box. The flowers are modest but plentiful, crowded in short clusters composed of both male and female flowers. Interest comes from the white sepals (there are no petals) and long stamens of the male blooms, also, in due course, from the round fleshy berries, which in some seasons hang alongside the following season's blooms. Sarcococcas do well in the shade in any moist but lime-free soil and increase readily from half-ripe summer cuttings. A rich, penetrating scent is their greatest attribute, with one added bonus for flower arrangers – the cut stems last weeks in water.

Sarcococca confusa, the tallest species, normally grows as a densely branched shrub. A plant in my garden, however, has become a 6 ft (1.8 m) bushy standard, presumably because I have kept its lower branches from developing so that ferns and hellebores have room to spread underneath. From late January to the end of February I am aware it is in flower from 10 yd (9 m) away, so strong is the honey scent of the flowers. The berries are black.

S. ruscifolia, a much shorter shrub of 2–4 ft (60–120 m), grows more erect, again has milk-white flowers, but has crimson berries.

Most people know summer-flowering climbing honeysuckles, but not all are aware that there are also winter-blooming bush types. Admittedly these are less showy and can be disappointing when the fragile blossoms are cut by spring frosts but, given a sheltered position and a mild winter, good quality, sweetly scented blooms are produced, followed later by crops of red, yellow, blue, white, or black berries.

Among the best of the winter varieties is the Chinese *Lonicera fragrantissima*, which will grow in most soils, in light to medium shade. The stems are upright, spreading with age to 6 ft (1.8 m) or 8 ft (2.4 m), but almost leafless in winter. Bunches of small, creamy-white, sweetly scented flowers appear in mild spells from late autumn until mid-spring. In a good year these will be succeeded by bunches of red fruits. *L. standishii*, a similar but inferior species, is sometimes grown as a wall shrub for the sake of its very fragrant white flowers. Both plants are easily propagated from hardwood cuttings in late summer.

Mahonias are evergreen shrubs related to berberis but vastly superior to that genus. The foliage, on stout main stems, is large and shiny, pinnate, with many leaflets, often terminating in sharp teeth. They thus differ considerably from *Berberis* species, which have teasing stem spines and small, simple leaves. The flowers, too, are more spectacular, being grouped in clusters on erect rounded spikes 4–8 in (10–20 cm) in length (longer in some species), which emanate near the tops of the stems, surrounded – like the arms of an octopus – by a circle of leaves.

The deliciously fragrant flowers of the winter-blooming Chinese honeysuckle, *Lonicera fragrantissima*

Although not as hardy as berberis, mahonias thrive in sheltered positions, being happy in any good garden soil and surprisingly tolerant of overhead shade from trees. However, they appear to best advantage when grown as specimen shrubs in an open border. The winter-blooming kinds are in great demand by connoisseurs, particularly species of Asiatic origin such as *Mahonia japonica* and *M. bealei*, both of which have stout spikes of yellow flowers with a lily-of-the-valley fragrance. The two species are often confused by growers, although the former is generally reckoned the best, with racemes sometimes 10 in (25 cm) in length, and leaves 12–18 in (30–45 cm) long. Although widely grown in Japan, it is not a Japanese native; in fact its country of origin is not known.

Other good winter bloomers are the erect-growing, 10–12 ft (3–3.6 m) high *M. lomariifolia* from China, which has rich, bright yellow flowers and pinnate leaves sometimes 2 ft (60 cm) long; a many-flowered hybrid from this species called 'Charity', softer yellow in colour; and an outstanding form called 'Lionel Fortescue', which has dense groups of branched spikes up to 16 in (40 cm) long with fragrant yellow flowers.

BELOW:
Mahonia lomariifolia 'Charity', an impressive winter bloomer with fragrant flowers borne on showy spikes

PAGES 146–7
LEFT:
Daphne mezereum, a good, hardy, winter-flowering shrub

RIGHT:
An early-flowering crocus, *Crocus chrysanthus*, to mark the end of winter

Most daphnes possess fragrant flowers, but few are winter-blooming. A worthwhile exception is the hardy mezereon (*Daphne mezereum*), a deciduous shrub, 2–4 ft (60–120 cm) tall, with erect branches bearing clusters of very fragrant, purplish-red flowers before the leaves in February and March, or even earlier in a mild winter. Later, bright red, currant-like berries develop, harmless to greenfinches and a few other birds but dangerous for man and most animals.

Mezereons are European plants, at one time being found wild in English woodlands. They are generally propagated by seeds, which if stored beforehand take two years to germinate, but when sown immediately after gathering usually come up the following spring. Half-ripe cuttings taken in July will root in sandy soil in a frame. There are varieties with different shades of pink flowers and 'Bowles' White' is an excellent albino form.

Winter is not a good season for herbaceous perennials unless their soft growth can be protected from the worst of the elements. Wind, frost, snow, and lashing rains all damage fragile flowers, although with the aid of a greenhouse or a light window indoors, spring and even summer can be anticipated and fragrant-flowering bulbs of hyacinths, paper-whites and other scented narcissi, and a variety of lilies can be raised for home enjoyment.

The heavily perfumed *Jasminum polyanthum* produces masses of white flowers in January and February but is not hardy. It can however be trained over a wire frame in a large flower pot of rich soil, or can be given a permanent position in a sun room or conservatory. Outdoors in mid-January the early flowering, honey-scented *Crocus chrysanthus* also makes an appearance and sweet violets bloom in frames or under cloches.

But one plant will survive outdoors, although those who grow it in their gardens generally live to regret it. It is really rampageous and suitable only for hedgerows and wild garden areas, but, given a suitable position, the early-flowering, sweetly scented winter helio-trope *Petasites fragrans* never fails to please. Belonging to the daisy family, it produces in February oval bunches of lilac-purple flowers with deep purple anthers on 4–8 in (10–20 cm) stems. The leaves are rounded, up to 8 in (20 cm) across, appearing in spring and in such quantities as to make a heavy ground cover. Sometimes these hang on until the following year.

SCENTED RECIPES

The garden of Pusey House, Wiltshire

MAKING A POMANDER

Take a thin-skinned orange and carefully cut and remove a narrow section of peel all round the fruit in two directions, thus making four quarters. Stud the remaining orange peel closely with cloves, using a bodkin or similar instrument if they are difficult to insert. Then roll the fruit in a bag containing equal parts of cinnamon and orris powder, repeating this frequently until it is completely coated. Stored in a warm, dry atmosphere it should be ready in five or six weeks. Dust off the surplus powder, tie a narrow ribbon round the cut-out areas of peel and hang the pomander in a wardrobe.

MAKING A POT-POURRI

There are dozens of recipes for pot-pourri. All the flowers and leaves must be gathered on a dry day. Green flower parts and the white heels of roses should be discarded, and the rest spread out on sieves or newsprint in an airy but shaded place to dry. Blend the ingredients subtly so that very powerful scents do not overwhelm the others and make the pot-pourri lose its gentle flower-scent characteristics.

Fixatives will be necessary to 'hold' the perfume. They may be of either plant or animal origin.

The most popular of the plant fixatives is orris powder. Use one tablespoon (15 ml) to a quart (1 l) of dried flowers. Calamus, which comes from the rhizome of the sweet flag (*Acorus calamus*), is also used.

The most commonly used animal fixatives are ambergris, which comes from the alimentary canal of spermaceti whales and is usually found floating in the sea; civet, which comes from glands under the tails of civet cats; and musk, which is obtained from the glands of the musk deer. Musk should be used very sparingly, or it will dominate the mixture – 1 drop of musk in 10 drops of alcohol, sprinkled over the dry ingredients, is the recommended quantity.

MAKING A DRY POT-POURRI

Mix well together the crisply dry petals, flowers, or leaves of roses, balm, sweet marjoram, bay, southernwood, rosemary, lavender, carnations, and lemon verbena, and rub everything to powder. Add at discretion pounded cloves, musk, and orris root.

ANOTHER POT-POURRI RECIPE

Placc dried rose petals and the flowers of mock orange, carnations, honeysuckle, and lavender (equal quantities of each) in a large bowl. Add dried leaves of sweet briar, lemon verbena, balm, rosemary, sweet marjoram, scented geranium, and southernwood. The proportions should be about one part of leaves to four parts of flowers. Mix together and add the dried powdered rind of a lemon and an orange, 1 oz (25 g) orris root, and half a tablespoonful (2.5 ml) each of allspice, ground cloves, and cinnamon, plus a pinch of powdered nutmeg and a pinch of sandalwood. Mix again.

Take a large jar and put a 2 in (5 cm) layer of the mixture in the base, sprinkle it with salt, add another layer of mixture and more salt, continuing thus until the jar is full. Cover tightly and leave for a week, apart from thoroughly stirring the mix once a day.

To make the scent stronger add a few drops of oil of cloves, oil of bergamot, and a few teaspoonfuls of eau de Cologne or lavender water. Fill small bowls with the finished mixture, and stir these occasionally to release the fragrance. Never put pot-pourri or perfume in plastic bottles or bowls however, or they will leach out the fragrance. An old pot-pourri can sometimes be revived by adding eight to ten drops of brandy, stirring well, and sealing it tightly for several days.

TO ENCOURAGE SLEEP
An old recipe from *Ram's Little Dodoen* (1606)

Take drie rose leaves, keep them close in a glasse which will keep them sweet, then take powder of mints, powder of cloves in a grosse powder. Put the same with the rose leaves, then put all these together in a bag, and take that to bed with you, and it will cause you to sleepe, and it is good to smell unto at other times.

A MOTH DETERRENT

Dry leaves of rosemary, mint, thyme, and tansy until they crumble, then mix 2 oz (50 g) each of the rosemary and mint with 1 oz (25 g) each of tansy and culinary thyme. Store the mixture in an airtight box, and when required scatter among blankets and clothes as a deterrent to moths and other insects.

MAKING PEACE PILLOWS

These make delightful gifts, particularly for invalids or elderly people. They are made by placing mixtures of dried scented leaves, flowers, and spices into a muslin bag or cushion cover, stitching the edges together, and fastening ribbons at the top corners so that the pillow can be hung over the back of a favourite chair. Leaning against the pillow releases the sweet fragrance, causing drowsiness and charming away the vilest headache. Particularly recommended ingredients are dried hop flowers, rose petals, lemon verbena, mint leaves, lavender, thyme, grated orange peel, allspice, cinnamon, sweet-geranium leaves, and orris powder. All should be well rubbed and mixed before inclusion.

LAVENDER WATER
From a recipe book of *c.* 1813

Suitable for hair washes, baths or to scent rooms.
Spirits of wine 1 quart
Oil of lavender ½ oz
Essence of ambergris ¼ oz
Essence of bergamot ½ oz
A few drops of musk if obtainable

Put in a bottle and shake well together. Leave several months to mature before using.

SCENTED ROSARY BEADS
A 19th-century recipe

Gather flowers of scented roses on a dry day; remove petals and chop these very finely. Place in a saucepan, barely cover with water and heat for about an hour without letting the mixture boil. Repeat for three days adding more water if necessary. Dark beads intended for rosaries are made this colour by warming them in a rusty saucepan. Never let the mixture boil. Mould the beads by working the pulp with the fingers and when well mixed and fairly dry force them on to a bodkin to make the holes. Work them about repeatedly on the bodkin or they may break if left until dry and rigid. Thread and when held in a warm hand for a few moments they will release a pleasant fragrance.

A SELECTION OF
FRAGRANT PLANTS

Syringa vulgaris, Common lilac

BOTANICAL NAME	COMMON NAME	SCENT

WINTER-BLOOMING PLANTS

Azara dentata	azara	sweet
Chimonanthus praecox	wintersweet	violet
Crocus chrysanthus	crocus	primrose
Daphne mezereum	mezereon	violet
Hamamelis mollis &		
varieties	witch hazel	strong violet
Lonicera fragrantissima,		
L. standishii	winter honeysuckle	honey
Mahonia japonica,		
M lomariifolia, & hybrids	hollygrape	sweet
Petasites fragrans	winter heliotrope	sweet
Viburnum farreri & other		
species	viburnum	rich

LAWN SUBSTITUTES

Anthemis nobilis	chamomile	very fragrant
Calamintha acinos (Acinos		
alpinus)	calamint	minty
Mentha requienii	Corsican mint	crème-de-menthe
Thymus serpyllum &		
varieties	lemon thyme	pungent aromatic

FRAGRANT HOUSE PLANTS

Cytisus canariensis	genista	softly fragrant
Gardenia jasminoides	Cape jasmine	richly fragrant
Jasminum polyanthum	jasmine	jasmine
Pelargonium scented-leaved		
species and varieties	geranium	rose, ginger
Primula malacoides	fairy primrose	primrose
Stephanotis floribunda	Madagascar jasmine	rich

NIGHT-SCENTED PLANTS

Heliotropium arborescens	cherry pie	spicy
Hesperis matronalis	dame's violet	clove
Matthiola bicornis	night-scented stock	clove
Nicotiana alata	tobacco plant	sweet
Oenothera biennis	evening primrose	vanilla

BOTANICAL NAME	COMMON NAME	SCENT

PLANTS FRAGRANT AFTER DRYING

Acorus calamus	sweet flag	(rhizome) aromatic
Dictamnus albus	burning bush	(seed heads) aromatic
Galium odoratum (*Asperula odorata*)	woodruff	(leaves) hay
Iris florentina	orris root	(rhizome) violet

AROMATIC ROOTS OR BARK

Asarum canadense	wild ginger	ginger
Iris florentina	orris	violet
Glycyrrhiza glabra	licorice, sweetwood	licorice
Sedum roseum (*S. rhodiola*)	roseroot	roses

SHRUBS WITH SCENTED LEAVES

Artemisia arbrotanum	old man, lad's love, southernwood	lemon
Cistus ladanifer, *C. laurifolius*	laudanum	sweetly aromatic
Lippia citriodora (*Aloysia triphylla*)	lemon verbena	lemon

SCENTED PLANTS FOR WINDOW BOXES AND OTHER CONTAINERS

Antirrhinum majus varieties	snapdragon	sweet
Calendula officinalis varieties	pot marigold	pungent
Lilium species and varieties	lilies	richly fragrant
Lobularia maritima	sweet alyssum	hay
Matthiola incana varieties	stocks	rich clove
Nicotiana × *sanderae*	tobacco plant	sweet
Reseda odorata	mignonette	sweet and strong
Tropaeolum majus varieties	nasturtium	sweet

SCENTED FLOWERS FOR CUTTING

Alstroemeria ligtu hybrids	Peruvian lily	mignonette
Calendula officinalis	pot marigold	pungent
Cheiranthus cheiri	wallflower	rich

BOTANICAL NAME	COMMON NAME	SCENT
Chrysanthemum	chrysanthemum	resinous
Hyacinthus	hyacinth	balsamic
Iris germanica	bearded iris	fruity
I. unguicularis	Algerian iris	softly sweet
Lathyrus odoratus varieties	sweet pea	sweet vanilla
Lilium regale and others	regal lily	rich and penetrating
Narcissus, many species and varieties	narcissus	jonquil
Paeonia lactiflora	paeony	rose
Rosa, many species and varieties	rose	varied, from delicate to rich and aromatic
Tropaeolum majus varieties	nasturtium	sweet spicy

SCENTED PLANTS FOR THE WATER GARDEN

Acorus calamus	sweet flag	aromatic
Aponogeton distachyus	water hawthorn	hawthorn
Cotula coronopifolia	brass buttons	lemon
Houttuynia cordata		orange
Mentha aquatica	water mint	aromatic
Mimulus ringens	Allegheny musk	minty
Nymphaea odorata forms, also tropical species and varieties	water lilies	very sweet and strong
Preslia cervina	preslia	minty

SCENTED PLANTS FOR SUN LOUNGES AND GREENHOUSES

Acacia dealbata	mimosa, silver wattle	spicy
Exacum affine	German violet	sweetly fragrant
Hoya carnosa	wax plant, porcelain flower	honey
Humea elegans	incense plant	incense
Jasminum polyanthum	jasmine	sweet, penetrating
Nerium oleander	oleander	soft, sweet
Pittosporum tobira	tobira	orange, penetrating

BOTANICAL NAME	COMMON NAME	SCENT
Plumbago capensis	Cape plumbago	heliotrope
Primula malacoides	fairy primrose	primrose
Stephanotis floribunda	Madagascar jasmine	rich

SCENTED PLANTS FOR WALLS OR FENCES

Akebia quinata	fiveleaf akebia	sweet
Clematis montana forms	mountain clematis	soft cowslip
Jasminum officinale	jasmine	jasmine
Lonicera japonica	Japanese honeysuckle	gardenia
L. periclymenum	woodbine	honey
Passiflora caerulea	passion flower	soft
Rosa, many climber species and varieties	rose	rose
Wisteria sinensis	Chinese wisteria	vanilla

LIME-TOLERANT SCENTED PLANTS

Iris germanica	bearded iris	fruity
Osmanthus delavayi	osmanthus	vanilla
Philadelphus californica and many others	mock orange	rich, sweet
Poncirus trifoliata	hardy orange	orange
Skimmia japonica	skimmia	rich, penetrating
Syringa vulgaris	lilac	sweet, rich
Viburnum carlesii, V. farreri and others	viburnum	clove

PLANTS WITH UNPLEASANT SCENT

Arum many species	arum, lords and ladies	nauseating
Dracunculus vulgaris	dragon plant	fetid
Fritillaria imperialis	crown imperial	foxy
Helicodiceros muscivorus	twist-arum	rotten flesh
Helleborus foetidus	setterwort, stinking hellebore	putrid
Lysichitum americanum	skunk cabbage	animal smell
Stapelia, various greenhouse succulent species	carrion flower	putrid

HARDY PLANTS AND SHRUBS WITH SCENTED LEAVES

BOTANICAL NAME	COMMON NAME	SCENT
Geranium macrorrhizum		aromatic
Mentha species and varieties	mints	minty
Rosmarinus officinalis	rosemary	pungent
Salvia, most species, especially *S. officinalis*	sage	pungent or aromatic
Santolina chamaecyparissus	cotton lavender	pungent
Thymus, most species	thyme	pine or lemon

INDEX

Page numbers in *italics* refer to illustrations.

A

Abeliophyllum distichum 140–42
Abies balsamea 35–6
achilleas *25*, 126, *129*
Akabia quinata 120
alecost 126
alstroemerias 110
alyssum, sweet 98
angelica 43
antirrhinums 104
artemisias *25*, 35, 132–5
Aruncus dioicus 90
azaleas 56–8
azaras 142–3

B

Bacon, Francis 28
Barnsley House *42*
Barr, Peter 62
bergamot 94, 126, *128*
bladdernut *33*
bluebells 62
bog myrtle 35, 80
Bowles, E. A. 33, 55, 62, 65, 78, 140
box *19*, 33
bugbane 33
burning bush *91*, 94

C

calamint 43
camellias 58, 138
camphor plant *126*
Capel Manor *60*
carnations 14, 94
catchfly, sweet-scented 98, *100–101*
catmint *95*, 96
chamomile 43, 97
Cheops, pharaoh 10
cherry, flowering 50
cherry pie 104
chestnuts, horse 74
China, ancient 13
Chinese orange 55
chrysanthemums 126
cinnamon 12–13

clematis 33, *115, 116*, 118–20
Cleopatra 22
Coats, Alice 50, 86
costmary 126
Cotoneaster frigida 33
cotton lavender 43, 96
cowslips 33, 66
cranesbill 96
Crinum × *powellii* 122, *123*
crocuses 62, 122, *147*, 148
crown imperial 62–5
Culpeper, Nicholas 135
currants, flowering 53–4
cyclamens 122–6
cypresses 35–6

D

daphnes *138, 146*, 148
daylilies 90–94
Dillenius, Johann 51
dogwoods 58, *60*
Dracunculus vulgaris 33

E

Egypt, ancient 10
Elaeagnus pungens 131, *132*
Elagabalus 23
elders 74, *75*
Elizabeth I 24, 26
Escallonia macrantha 118
eucalyptus 35
evening primrose 29, *30–31*, 70, 107

F

feverfew *121*, 126, *127*
Fortune, Robert 20
Fothergilla gardenii 51–3
frangipani 29
frankincense 10–12
freesias 28

G

Galega officinalis 104
gardenias 29
geraniums, scented *34*, 35
Gerard, John 66, 78
germander 129, *130*

gladioli 110, 122, *124–5*
goat's rue *102*, 104
gorse 50–51
Greeks, ancient 22, 24

H

Hatsheput, queen of Egypt 10
Haworth-Booth, Michael 139–40
hawthorns 33, 72–4
heathers 54, 138
Helicodiceros 32, 33
heliotrope, winter 33, 148
hellebores *60*, 138
Hibberd, James Shirley 20
Hillier, Sir Harold 54
hollyhocks 129
honeysuckles 29, 58, *60*, 70, 114–15, 143–4
hostas 110
hyacinths 28, 58, *61*, 148
   grape *61*, 62
   summer 107, *113*
hyssop 129

I

incense 10, 12
irises *16*, 17, 36, 62, 86
   bearded 86, *87*

J

jasmines 115–18, *134*, 135–6, 148
Jekyll, Gertrude 20

K

Kalm, Peter 51
Kingdon Ward, Frank 51
knot gardens 17, *42*

L

laurel, Californian 78
   bay 78–80
lavender *25*, 35, 43, 96
Libocedrus decurrens 35–6
lilacs *76*, 77, 120
lilies 28, 72, 107–10, *111*, 148
   madonna 17, *40*, 108

lilies of the valley 47, 65–6, *67*
limes 74
Linnaeus, Carolus 51
Lobb, William 20
Loudon, J. C. and Mrs J. W. 20
lupins 98–104
Lychnis chalcedonica 39

M

magnolias 33, 48–50, 78
mahonias 58, 144–5
marigolds 33, 98, *103*
marvel of Peru 29, *32*
meadowsweet *24*, 33
Mexican orange 58, *59*
mezereons 148
Michaux, André 78
mignonettes 104
mints 43, 80, 98, 126
mock orange 28, 70, *71*, 77–8, *79*
monardas 94, 126, *128*
Muhammad 13
musk, scented 138
myrrh 10

N

Napoleon I 68
narcissi 7, 62, *63*, 148
nasturtiums 104, *107*
Nepeta × *faassenii* 129–131
Nerine bowdenii 122
Nero 14, 23
Newby Hall *41*

O

Oenothera missouriensis 109
orange, hardy *56*
orris *16*, 17, 86
Osmanthus 54–5, 131

P

paeonies 85–6, *88–9*
pansies 66
   winter 138
Parkinson, John 24, 66, 126
passion flower 136
Paxton, Joseph 20

Perovskia atriplicifolia 132, *133*
Peruvian lily *112*
petunias 107
phlox 33, 94
Picea 35–6
pinks *92*, 94
poached-egg flower 104, *106*
polyanthuses 66
Poncirus trifoliata 56
poplars 50
pot marigolds 104
potentilla *25*
primroses 66
privet 28

Q
queen of the night 29

R
rhododendrons 56
Robinson, William 20, 138
rocket, sweet 98
Romans, ancient 14, 22–4
rosemary *18*, *21*, 35, 43, 80

Rosengarten, Frederic 13
roseroot 36
roses 22–4, *39*, 80–82, *83*, *84*
    climbing 82; floribunda 82,
    83; hybrid tea 82–5;
    musk 82; *Rosa damascena*
    17; *R. gallica 9*, *15*, *81*, 82,
    83; *R. g. officinalis* 14;
    Rosa mundi *83*; *R. rugosa*
    82; shrub 82
Royal Horticultural Society
    20, *41*

S
Sackville West, Vita 126
saffron 14, 17
sage *40*, 43, 96, *97*, 129
Sahure, pharaoh 10
sarcococcas 58, *142*, 143
savory, 129
    winter *130*
Sheba, queen of 12
Shen Nung, emperor 13
skimmias 74–7

Smith, Sir James E. 50–51
snapdragons 104
snowdrops 17, 62
snowflake, spring 62
Solomon 12
southernwood *25*, 35, 132–5
Spanish broom 131–2
spices 17
Stapelia 33
Staphylea colchica 33
Stern, F. C. 62
stocks 29, 70, *90*, 104, *105*
sweet bay 35
sweet flag *119*
sweet gale 35
sweet pea 98, *99*
sweet sultan 98
sweet william *69*, *93*, 94
Sybaris 24

T
Thebes, gardens at 10
Thomas, Graham 94
thymes 43, 80, 97

tobacco plant 29, 70, 107, 108
tuberose *28*, 29

V
verbena, lemon 35, 80, *81*, 131
viburnums *52*, 53, 138–9
Victoria, queen 20
violet, sweet 68
violet cress 104

W
wallflowers 66–8
water lilies *27*, *35*, 70
    giant *19*, 20
Waterperry 40
wattles 29, 55
Wilson, E. II. 107
wintersweet 139–40
Wisley garden 41
wisteria *117*, 120
witch hazel 140, *141*

Y
yuccas 110–14